MYTHS IN THE OLD TESTAMENT

MYTHS IN
THE OLD TESTAMENT

Benedikt Otzen   Hans Gottlieb
Knud Jeppesen

SCM PRESS LTD

Translated by Frederick Cryer from the Danish
Myter i Det gamle Testamente
published by G. E. C. Gads Forlag, Copenhagen
2nd edition, 1976

334 01050 0

First published in English 1980
by SCM Press Ltd
58 Bloomsbury Street, London WC1

Printed in Great Britain by
Billing & Sons Ltd, Guildford and Worcester

To Professor Erling Hammershaimb

CONTENTS

FOREWORD

The Scandinavian school has long been a challenging and stimulating influence in Old Testament studies, sharing many points of view with the English 'Myth and Ritual' approach. For the English reader unfamiliar with any of the Scandinavian languages it is difficult, however, to gain a proper impression of the richness and variety of approaches and results of this school, since most of the scholars belonging to it write in their own native tongue only. The studies here translated are therefore particularly welcome. They deal with a central theme, myth, and are not only representative of the approach of the Scandinavian school, particularly in its Danish form, but their usefulness generally is greatly enhanced by the conscientiousness with which the authors present their views against a broad background of reference to, and evaluation of, theories of others, mostly of course, Scandinavians, but other European scholars too.

The book begins with a clear and informative discussion of the term 'myth', tracing its history in Old Testament scholarship, distinguishing it from saga (sagn) and fairy tale, and finally limiting it, for purposes of the studies presented, to the meaning 'cult myth'. This, though it may seem a bit narrow to an English reader, does make for clarity and consistency and avoids the often confusing multiplicity of meanings of the term in English.

Next follows a chapter on myth in Genesis in which the rigour of the definition adopted fortunately does not prevent a detailed and enlightening discussion of the accounts of creation, the fall, and the flood with evaluation of the many and varied attempts at explanation that have been offered through the years, even though, – as a bow to the definition – they can be accorded only a 'basis' in the mythical world view and not accepted as true 'myths'.

The following chapter, on myth in the Psalms, treats of the creation myth, Yahweh's victory over Leviathan, with the myths of the exodus from Egypt, the battle with the nations, the enthronement of Yahweh and the mythology surrounding the figure of the king.

Lastly, myth in the prophets is considered in a discussion of themes such as judgment and salvation, death and resurrection, sacred marriage and the development from royal ideology to messianic expectations.

The reader will be likely, we should think, to read these studies with disagreement as often as with agreement, but also, surely, with delight in an urbane, informative and lucid presentation which cannot but stimulate to independent thinking.

Harvard, 1979   *Professor Thorkild Jacobsen*

PREFACE

The Danish book *Myter i Det gamle Testamente*, on which this English edition is based, was first published in 1973 (2nd ed. 1976). In some cases references have been altered to accommodate English speaking readers, but only in a few cases have they been brought up to date.

We should like to express our gratitude to Professor Thorkild Jacobsen, who suggested the English edition and kindly consented to write a foreword, and to Professor James Barr, who helpfully established contact with SCM Press, and who also generously took upon himself to read a proof, and made very valuable suggestions.

Benedikt Otzen
Hans Gottlieb
Knud Jeppesen

ABBREVIATIONS

AcOr	*Acta Orientalia*, Leiden
AJSL	*American Journal of Semitic Languages and Literatures*, Chicago
ANET	*Ancient Near Eastern Texts relating to the Old Testament*, ed. J. B. Pritchard, Princeton ^{3}1969
ATD	Das Alte Testament Deutsch, Göttingen
AV	Authorized Version of the Bible
BJRL	*Bulletin of the John Rylands Library*, Manchester
BKAT	Biblischer Kommentar. Altes Testament, Neukirchen
BZAW	Beihefte zur *Zeitschrift für die alttestamentliche Wissenschaft*, Berlin
DTT	*Dansk teologisk Tidsskrift*, Copenhagen
ET	English translation
EvTh	*Evangelische Theologie*, Munich
HAT	Handbuch zum Alten Testament, Tübingen
HUCA	*Hebrew Union College Annual*, Cincinnati
ICC	International Critical Commentary, Edinburgh and New York
IDB Suppl	*Interpreter's Dictionary of the Bible*, Supplementary Volume, New York 1976
NEB	New English Bible, Oxford and Cambridge 1970
NERT	*Near Eastern Religious Texts relating to the Old Testament*, ed. W. Beyerlin, ET London and Philadelphia 1978
NT	New Testament
NTT	*Norsk teologisk tidsskrift*, Oslo
OT	Old Testament
OTL	Old Testament Library, London and Philadelphia
RGG^3	*Die Religion in Geschichte und Gegenwart*, Tübingen ^{3}1956–65
RHPR	*Revue d'histoire et de philosophie religieuses*, Strasbourg
RoB	*Religion och Bibel*, Stockholm

RSV　　　　　　Revised Standard Version of the Bible, London and New York 1946

SBT　　　　　　Studies in Biblical Theology, London and Naperville

SBU　　　　　*Svenskt bibliska uppslagsverk*, Stockholm

SEÅ　　　　　*Svenskt exegetisk årsbok*, Lund

StTh　　　　　*Studia Theologica*, Lund

SVT　　　　　　Supplements to *Vetus Testamentum*, Leiden

TDOT　　　　*Theological Dictionary of the Old Testament*, ed. G. J. Botterweck and H. Ringgren, ET Grand Rapids, Michigan 1974ff.

VT　　　　　　*Vetus Testamentum*, Leiden

1

THE CONCEPT OF MYTH

Benedikt Otzen

Myth and theology

It was not until the age of the Romantics that myth began to come into its own in Western thought and culture. Previously, of course, both the ancient Greek and Nordic myths had been known; but either they were interpreted as examples of corrupt historiography in which the gods appeared as reflections of prehistoric heroes, or the old myths were considered to be nature allegories and the gods seen as personifications of such natural phenomena as lightning, thunder, rain, and so forth. In the Enlightenment, in the latter part. of the eighteenth century, people in the more learned circles began to interest themselves in myth, and a little later again, under the influence of the Romantic philosophy of identity – here Schelling comes to mind – myth achieves a special significance, according to which it becomes a symbol of the eternal which lives in man, and of which man is an emanation.[1] Such thoughts were set forth in a both remarkable and original way during the first decades of the nineteenth century by the Danish priest, poet, and historian, N. F. S. Grundtvig.[2] Grundtvig's imposing view of Nordic mythology gave to myth a central position in the Nordic consciousness. As a youth, Grundtvig had read Schelling and come to realize the nature of myth as neither inferior historiography nor nature allegory; rather, it was a superb expression of man's spiritual experience. It was a record of the Northman's soul, of the 'Nordic giant spirit' which perhaps reposed in sleep, but which might be reawakened by reanimating the message of the myths – a task which Grundtvig understood as his.

By means of a highly subjective and 'existential' interpretation of the Nordic myths, Grundtvig worked out a comprehensive view of myth as a 'picture of human life throughout the whole of history'. The central elements of Nordic mythology, he felt, were the struggle between the Æsir (gods) and the Giants, the 'twilight of the gods' in Ragnarok, and the resurrection of the gods to new life with the All-Father in Gimle [the Nordic 'abode of the blessed']. Similarly, according to Grundtvig, man's existence (by 'man' he meant both the individual and the race) is a battle of life against death, but also a battle which leads man towards eternity and to acceptance of divine life.

This understanding of myth was above all of significance for Grundtvig's pedagogical theories, which were to be realized in the Danish Folk High School. His ideas, however, exercised only indirect influence upon Scandinavian theological thought and research in the nineteenth century. Outside Denmark, theological and philosophical interest in myth was, as we noted above, strong in the Romantic period. But the attempt in the 1830s by the German scholar D. F. Strauss to comprehend the entire New Testament as myth seems to have made contemporary theologians uneasy about the concept. Accordingly, this line of interpretation was not prominent throughout the rest of the century.[3] Researchers in the history of religions and folklore, however, who became active in the latter half of the nineteenth century, preserved an interest in myth. Their method was essentially an attempt to get behind a particular myth and expose its nature. In fact, it was thanks to research into the history of religions that myth again became significant for theology.

At the turn of the century, myth still played only a modest role in theology. If we were to consult the then most important German theological encyclopædia, the twenty-four-volume *Realenzyklopädie für protestantische Theologie und Kirche* (1896–1913), in which virtually all of the period's theological knowledge is represented, we would search in vain for an article on 'myth' or 'mythology'. The same is true of the English *Encyclopædia Biblica* (1899–1907), in which we otherwise find collected the results of nineteenth-century biblical research.

But in the first decades of the twentieth century, the picture changes. Biblical research was now dominated by the influence of the 'history of religions school', and we find myth taking a leading place in both Old and New Testament research. In this period it was usual to emphasize the strong connections between the accounts of the OT primeval history and the oriental myths which recent excavations had brought to scholarly attention. As far as the New Testament was concerned, it was common to assert the importance of Hellenistic and gnostic conceptions for the articulation of the New Testament message. There is a direct line of continuity from this hermeneutical tradition to the post-war controversy centred on Rudolf Bultmann, who demanded that the New Testament kerygma be 'demythologized', in order to make it accessible to modern man.

The concept of myth received a new formulation in the context of the debate about demythologizing:

> Mythology is the use of imagery to express the other-worldly in terms of this world and the divine in terms of human life, the other side in terms of this side. . . It expresses man's understanding of himself in the world in which he lives. Myth should be interpreted not cosmologically, but anthropologically, or better still, existentially.[4]

Thus, according to Bultmann, the myths of the New Testament talk about things in the beyond in an objective way, which is meaningless to 'modern man' whose canons of perception have been determined by a 'scientific' understanding of the world. If the message of the NT is to speak to contemporary people, it must be rescued from 'the historically conditioned form of their mythological perceptions'. Interestingly, we here encounter the point of view which we already met in conjunction with Grundtvig's understanding of the heathen mythologies of Greece and the North: myth requires interpretation!

The question is, whether this also applies to the myths of the OT; do they also attempt to express more than they in fact say? In research the myths of the OT have not been given the same treatment as the NT myths have received. Rather, the central concern of OT research has been to lay bare the Israelite's understanding of the myths he appropriated from neighbouring countries. As mentioned above, we have in recent generations become aware that there exists a close relation between what we call myth in the OT writings and those myths with which we have become acquainted since it became possible in the latter part of the nineteenth century for us to read the cuneiform writings of Mesopotamia. It was quickly observed that there are astonishing similarities between the Mesopotamian myths and those of the OT, principally between the Babylonian creation epic Enuma Elish and the biblical creation narratives, and between the story of Gilgamesh and the biblical account of the flood. Moreover, it was readily apparent that any inquiry as to the primacy of one or other group of narratives – and it was obvious that there had to be a connection of some sort

– inevitably led to the Babylonian accounts, since they were so much older than their biblical counterparts.

The decisive question that emerged was concerned with the relationship between the foreign myths which Israel appropriated and Israel's own self-understanding, as expressed in the OT. One might suppose that it should be possible to point to a degree of tension between the religous forms of expression peculiar to Israel and those of the foreign mythology, or at least to a tension between the theology which was important to those circles who carried out the final redaction of the OT and that of the imported myths. This view is held by several scholars, who maintain that the OT offers evidence of a perpetual tendency to reject myth, or in some way to take exception to it.

However, there is also the possibility that a particular foreign myth was for Israel the best means of expressing something central to the concerns of Israelite religion, or, in other words, that Israel was able to interpret the myth in such a way that it became 'domesticated' and no longer was perceived as a body foreign to the OT. Before we press on in the investigation of these questions, it would be reasonable to determine more exactly just what a myth in fact is.

Myth, saga and fairy-tale

It is tempting to refer to Grundtvig again since he concerned himself so much with myth that we should expect to find a clear definition of the concept in his work. He did in fact make a number of attempts in this direction, of which the clearest is probably the following:

> Myth is a Greek name for pictorial language in the service of the spirit, or the 'winged word'; it is rightly used of the sagas about the gods, which are a people's pictorial language at its most beautiful.[5]

Grundtvig's definition is not far from that of a folklorist and researcher in the history of religions like Axel Olrik, who identifies myth with the 'god-myth', since, as he says, myth is not a 'formal definition, but a definition of content. It is a saga which has to do with supernatural events, and whose protagonist has superhuman abilities.'[6]

Definitions of this kind have played a leading part in the OT research of our century. The German Hermann Gunkel, who was the leading figure in the history of religions school, says concisely

'Myths are stories about the gods, in contradistinction to the sagas, whose active personae are human.'[7] Furthermore, Gunkel emphasizes that the myths or survivals of myths we have in the OT are primarily 'origin-sagas' or aetiologies, and that their purpose is to explain in what ways the gods' actions have been responsible for existing conditions in the human world. Thus they have the form of answers to the question 'Why?' Why are heaven and earth established as they are? Why is man composed of body and spirit? Why is the relationship between man and woman as it in fact is? Why is death the assured fate of all men? Myth thus gives answers to man's most basic and central questions.

Gunkel's definition is not wrong; it certainly points in the right direction, but fails none the less to be comprehensive. It is really concerned with the periphery of the phenomenon, and this means that the distinction between 'myth' and 'saga' remains too tenuous. It is clear that these two types of literature have a tendency to overlap each other's boundaries, but it would be advantageous if we could penetrate, for the sake of clarity, to the essential difference between them, and if we furthermore could delimit them in relation to such other narrative types as the fairy-tale, the legend, and so on.

It is in this area that more recent research into the history of religions and the OT has been active; scholars have especially concentrated their attention on the differing *concepts of time* which are characteristic of myth and saga. This has entailed a certain narrowing down of the concept of myth; at the same time, however, it has most certainly contributed to the illumination of the difference in question.[8]

We shall begin with the category of *saga*, which Olrik has defined as follows:

> By 'saga' is understood a report which represents something as an event which has taken place; the report goes from mouth to mouth without the various links in the chain being able to determine either the origin of the story or who its earlier tradents were.[9]

It is significant that Olrik, as a folklorist, places especial weight on the process of transmission of a saga; however, his definition is also insufficiently comprehensive. The Swedish scholar C.-M. Edsman comes closer to the heart of the matter when he asserts that a saga is a story which is regarded as true, the content of which is connected with space and time so that it refers to particular historical or mythical figures, events, or localities.[10] Edsman holds that the decisive aspect is that a saga has a certain basis in historical events and takes place, or at least pretends to do so, within historical space and time. Thus a saga adheres to a particular historical context and a definite geographical milieu. A saga attempts to be history.

At the same time, it is clear that it is of no significance that mythical or supernatural beings also figure in a saga. Both the Nordic and Greek heroic sagas are often localized both historically and geographically (a fact which says nothing at all about their credibility), while they at the same time very often refer to supernatural and divine figures. The boundaries between stories about the gods and heroic sagas are quite fluid; according to one Danish saga King Skjold lives in the town of Lejre, near Roskilde; in another he is a son of the god Odin. Matters are analogous in the patriarchal traditions of the OT, which deal with Abraham, Isaac, and Jacob: Abraham dwells in Mamre, near Hebron, and there is visited by divine personages, even by Yahweh himself. Likewise, in the country to the east of Jordan Jacob fights with what is either an angelic or a demonic being, and so on.

Further, what Gunkel said of myth applies also to saga: that its purpose is often explanatory. We meet this type of saga (aetiological or explanatory) in a number of cultures, and in great numbers in the OT. Thus a strange rock formation near the Dead Sea is explained by the saga about Lot's wife; the names of the primeval ancestors of Israel are explained by special features of their births; the origins of cult and holy places are explained by stories saying that the ancestral fathers once dwelt there and in such and such a place received divine revelation. Similarly, an oasis came into being in the midst of the desert because Moses struck the rock there with his staff. The saga has a function; it arises not just from the desire to tell a good story, but to give later generations understanding of the things which surround them.[11]

The *fairy-tale*, on the other hand, arose primarily to satisfy the ordinary human impulse to entertain, and to be entertained, by a good story. It is characteristic of the fairy-tale, in contrast to the saga, that it need have nothing to do with an historical course of events. The fairy-tale is timeless, as the characteristic introductory phrase 'Once upon a time . . . ', indicates.[12] The fairy-tale is not concerned with when or where its events occur, but only with the development of plot. Further, the fairy-tale is often strongly stylized and employs a repertoire of stock characters more often than it relies on individualized personae, just as the development of the story is often quite stereotyped (the three brothers who want to seek their fortune, the apparently poor and humble man who is raised to honour and glory, etc.). However, these stock characteristics may also appear in the saga, and the distinction between saga and fairy-tale is therefore often a difficult one to make. The migratory saga, for example (more or less identical tales which are told about different persons) has the aspect of a fairy-tale; it has acquired a fixed form and stereotypical features. To take an example: if we compare Gen. 12 with chs. 20 and 26, we find three stories which have been cut from the same cloth. The first two stories have to do with Sara, only in different situations, while the third features Rebecca. Undoubtedly, this story was much loved, so that it was told time and time again; just who were its *dramatis personae*, and where it all happened, however, seem to have been beside the point. The story was less a saga about the ancestors than a tale with a good moral attached to it.[13]

Finally, *legend*. Legend approximates to saga, but its distinctive characteristic is that it has an edifying thrust. The stories about the prophets Elijah and Elisha in the books of Kings and the remarkable narratives about Daniel in the first half of the book of Daniel all attempt to illustrate how Yahweh helps the man who trusts in him. In common with the saga, the legend is usually historically and geographically localized, despite the fact that most legends undoubtedly have no historical foundation.

If we then are to attempt to understand *myth* on the basis of what we have said above, that is, if we should attempt to discover the mythical concept of time, we must concentrate on the relation of myth to history. Here again it is characteristic that, unlike saga, myth has no base in history, nor does it in any case pretend to belong to the time and space of history. Myth exceeds the boundaries of history, and the events of which it speaks lie beyond the pale of real time, in which historical events occur. Myth has its own time, which may be designated mythical time; it consists of *Urzeit* and *Endzeit*, that which lies both before and after historical time.

This understanding of myth has become current in recent research in the history of religions. It is immediately obvious that the conception of myth thus formulated is considerably narrower than was that of Gunkel, who broadly described myths as 'stories about the gods'. As early as the 1930s, the Dutch scholar Gerardus van der Leeuw rejected Gunkel's definition, and maintained instead that myth parts company with the normal concept of time and partakes of eternity:

If nevertheless we attempt to fix it in time, we must place it either at the beginning or at the end of all happening, either in the primeval era or at the conclusion of time, that is before or after 'time'.[14]

Most religions contain a complex of ideas dealing with the 'first' and 'last' things, that is, they relate how things came into being and what will happen in the 'last times'. It is these conceptions which come into play in myth. There is as a rule a clear correspondence between the first and last things; the events of the last times are perceived as a return to the time of the beginning, which is the perfect and ideal time. For example, it is clear in both Jewish and Christian thought-worlds that there exists a close connection between the narratives of creation and paradise in Genesis, on the one hand, and the descriptions in the OT of the glorious future and the events described by the book of Revelation in the NT, on the other. Thus it is most important that we should understand the myth about the events of the *Urzeit* or primeval era.

Mircea Eliade has made an intensive study of myth and its relation to time and space, and specifically the myth of the primeval time.[15] He has written of the way 'primitive man', that is, the man who experiences his existence religiously, has two concepts of time. Ordinarily he lives in normal, profane, 'historical' time, which may be described as linear, and in which take place all the routine events with no specifically religious content. However, he also lives in 'sacred time'; it is packed with religious content which comes to expression in his religious feasts and ceremonies. Eliade finds that the distinctive characteristic of sacred time is that it is, as he says, *reversible*; that is, it constantly returns to its point of departure and thus runs in a circle, in contrast to profane time, which moves in a straight line. Thus Eliade insists that sacred time is in reality the mythical primeval time which intersects with profane time; the points of contact between sacred and profane time are the cultic feasts in which man experiences his existence religiously. This relationship may be illustrated graphically as we have done below. The horizontal line here signifies historical, profane time, a time which has its own beginning and end, but which is repeatedly intersected by ellipses which designate sacred time as a repetition of the primeval events which precede the beginning of history. The largest ellipse, which on the right-hand side goes beyond the horizontal line of profane time, represents the eschatological event of the end-time, which, as we said above, is perceived as a return to the conditions of the primeval time.

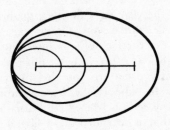

This understanding of time, says Eliade, is an expression of the need of religious man to become 'contemporary with the gods', his wish to return to 'a primordial situation, that in which the gods and the mythical ancestors were *present*, that is, were engaged in creating the world, or in organizing it, or in revealing the foundations of civilization to man'. Thus man desires 'to live in the world as it came from the Creator's own hands, fresh, pure, and strong'.[16]

The creation myth and the New Year Festival

The act of creation plays a central role in all of the previously depicted complexes of ideas. The concept 'act of creation' should here be construed in its widest possible sense; it has to do with the divine establishment of the cosmos, of the well-ordered world in which man lives (some scholars prefer the term 'myths of the beginning'). The notion that the primeval act, the creation which takes place outside time, breaks into history to become the present overlays the idea that the created world can be maintained only by being constantly renewed. The act of creation is repeated, and this repetition is a condition of the world's further subsistence, and the ground of man's confidence, in the teeth of everything that threatens his world. Moreover, not only is the world 'recreated', man himself is 'reborn' and thereby redeemed from all the hostile powers.

The idea of the repetition of the creation is connected with the New Year in quite a number of primitive religions, both ancient and modern. There are indeed few religions which have failed to observe the rhythm of the year and interpret it as an expression of enormous cosmic forces on which man is dependent. The annual cycle plays a thoroughly natural part in virtually every hunting and agricultural religion. Clearly, this fact explains the primitive fear that the regularity of the procession of the seasons will cease, and fertility and human existence thus be threatened.

The seasons of the year have differing qualities: certain seasons are favourable to life (the seasons of light, warmth, and rain), while other seasons are destructive of life (winter, the seasons of reduced light and of drought). It is precisely for this reason that the various phases of the yearly cycle are bounded by religious ceremonies, whose purpose is to support the regular order of things; more specifically, it is the season when time 'turns about' and the new year is created, that is attended by a fateful religious tension.[17] Further, the best way one can ensure the prosperity of the coming year is by repeating the primeval act of creation. The inauguration of the year is a cosmic event; if the cosmos is recreated, the yearly cycle is assured.

But what does the repetition of the primeval act of creation on the occasion of the New Year Festival entail? As we said above, it happens in the cultic actions performed in the course of the festival. To modern man a cultic action can never be other than a symbolic action, and indeed to many the cultic ceremony would be an empty symbol. However, the primitive, religiously thinking individual sees things in quite a different perspective; to him a cultic action may be the most powerful event in his existence. Again, to primitive man cult is a drama which creates both life and reality. Thus in the New Year Festival the fundamental primeval events are performed in dramatic enactment as a new reality. To this we should again object that a dramatic presentation can never be other than symbolic; and yet, it is clear that primitive man recognizes an identity between symbol and reality in a way we are scarcely able to grasp. He does not even require a dramatic enactment of the creation; rather, the essential properties may be as simple as a pictorial representation, or the recitation of a verbal account. What occurs in principle is a repetition which is experienced as a re-creation.

This whole conception can hardly find a better formulation than the following by Vilhelm Grønbech:

> In the cult, the world is born anew; it is the origin of all things. It therefore signifies a clean break with what we understand as the chronological time sequence. At each great festival we begin again from scratch, and as long as the festival lasts the door of time sags on its hinges. The festival is the focal point at which all the rays are concentrated and vanish, only to re-emerge

subsequently with renewed power and coherence. In consequence, the past itself, history, must be reanimated in the cult. The great deeds of the ancestors are worked through and become present and actual, often perhaps as a segment of the battle with the demons and in order to strengthen the people in their future combats, even as the creation of the earth and the origin of the human race are dramatically suggested, because in the cultic event everything suddenly becomes the present. The correspondences we everywhere find between the creation myths of primitive peoples and the central activities of their cult demonstrate how real it all is to them. . . What the child experiences, when he awakens on Christmas morning and 'no longer counts the hours', is of a piece with the experiences of the primitive during the hours of the festival. The open, pliable, submissive nature which seems so weak and yet can shape everything, because it can enter into everything, this is the soul of the festival.[18]

Thus we return to *myth*. In the quotation above, Grønbech remarks that we can 'everywhere' observe a correspondence between the creation myth and the central actions of the cult. It is in this cultic context (depicted above) that myth has its function; it is myth that gives the cultic action its content and forms its drama.

Somewhat earlier we gave a preliminary definition of myth as that which represents an event which occurs outside historical space and time, in the primeval time or at the end of time. Now we can go a step further: it is also characteristic of myth that it is, in one way or another, bound to the cult. This perception has been strongly emphasized in the research of recent decades. Widengren goes so far as to say that the moment myth is separated from the cult it ceases to be myth and becomes instead either saga or legend: 'Myth describes the cultic ritual, and the cultic ritual lends impulsive force to the myth.'[19] Mowinckel puts it just as strongly:

A real myth is linked with the cult, has emerged from it, and expresses the fundamental events which happen and have happened, the salvific action which is 'recalled' in the cultic re-experience.[20]

To put it another way, primitive man experiences in the cult the reality which myth expresses. In this way the cult manages to erect a bridge between the suprahuman world outside space and time and the historical world of man. Again we approach Grundtvig's concept of the poetic, mythical, pictorial language that constitutes the 'shuddering bridge which connects heaven and earth'.[21]

Myth, however, does more than form the basis of cultic activity. Those actions of which myth speaks, and which occur outside the confines of the time and space and of human history, are sacred and fundamental; that is, they are determinative for man and his existence, and adumbrate the conditions under which man lives. In reality, myth becomes a vehicle for an explanation of existence; it expresses an understanding of life. Myth explains how the elementary relations of man's world came into being and why they are the way they are. This explanation of existence is not theoretical and abstract. Since primitive man encounters the content of myth in the cult, he meets the mythical explanation of existence as a living reality.[22]

What, then, is the relationship that obtains between a myth and the cult with which it is connected? This relationship is not unambiguous; it can be so simple that the two quantities are fused indissolubly together, but things can also be more complicated. To cite Grønbech again,

> They are such direct extensions of one another that myth merely explains the situation of the cult to us like the explanatory caption under a picture. However, the relationship between myth and cult is usually more complicated. It is true that myth always has to do with what happens in the cult, but quite often it goes its own way, since it is comprised of poetry about events whose influence can be felt in all of life's relations. It is therefore important to see myth as an entity in itself which provides the cult with its spiritual background.[23]

We have already noted that the creation myth enjoys a central position in most religions. If we take the concept of creation in its broadest possible construction, so that it covers everything that has to do with the establishment of the human world in the primeval era, we could claim that all true myths represent one or another side of the myth of creation, or are derived from it. Eliade puts this idea sharply:

> Myth proclaims the appearance of a new cosmic situation or of a primordial event. Hence it is always the recital of a creation; it tells how something was accomplished, began to be. . . Every myth shows how a reality came into existence, whether it be the total reality, the cosmos, or only a fragment – an island, a species of plant, a human institution.[24]

The same point of view comes to the fore in the typological analysis of myth which has been carried out in one of the most recent studies in the phenomenology of religion by the German scholar, Friedrich Heiler:

1. Theogonic myths: narratives concerning the origins of the gods.

2. Cosmogonic myths: accounts of the creation of the world, the establishment of the cosmos and subjugation of chaos.

3. Cosmological myths: explanations of the order of nature as a divine statute anchored in the primeval era; to this category belong also solar, astral, and seasonal myths.

4. Anthropological myths: narratives about the creation of man and his relationship with the gods; here belong also stories about the fall and the flood.

5. Ancestor myths: stories which depict the origins of a people or tribe; the nature of saga is such that this type comes very close to saga.

6. Cult myths: explanations of a cult ceremony, or the primeval origin of a sanctuary; these, too, verge on the genre of the saga.

7. Soteriological revelation myths or saviour myths: these depict divine intervention in the human world via the agency of a saviour; this category can scarcely be distinguished clearly from no. 9.

8. Myths about the beyond (*Jenseitsmythen*): narratives about the underworld and journeys to heaven, man's relationship to death, eternal life, and so on; these seem to belong together with the category of anthropological myths listed under no. 4.

9. Eschatological myths: the events of the end-time, the world cataclysm, and the re-establishment of the primal situation.[25]

The Babylonian myth of creation

Heiler's synopsis gives a useful survey of the world of myth, and with the reservations we have suggested one can easily sense that the myth of creation is the central datum. To avoid the feeling that our approach here is too abstract, it will be instructive to examine an actual creation myth, which may be taken to be typical. Since we shall encounter it again later in this work, we here choose the Babylonian myth as it appears in the epic *Enuma Elish*.[26] This poem was originally recited and was the basis of the cultic drama in the ceremonies of the Babylonian *Akitu* festival, the New Year Festival. The poem tells us about the primordial gods Tiamat, representing the sea, and Apsu, the divinity of fresh water. Together they beget a number of gods, but when these latter disturb the repose of the older gods, Apsu decides to annihilate them. Ea, one of the young gods, thereupon opposes Apsu and kills him. Tiamat creates an army of gruesome demoniac beings who with Kingu (her new husband) as leader introduce a reign of terror. Chaos rules among the gods, and chaos is, above all in the figure of Tiamat, represented by the menacing and destructive waters. Ea, however, gives birth to Marduk, who dares to take up the battle against the goddess of chaos, Tiamat:

> Then joined issue Tiamat and Marduk, wisest of gods.
> They strove in single combat, locked in battle.
> The lord spread out his net to enfold her,
> the Evil Wind, which followed behind, he let loose in her face.
> When Tiamat opened her mouth to consume him,
> he drove in the Evil Wind that she close not her lips.
> As the fierce winds charged her belly,
> her body was distended and her mouth was wide open.
> He released the arrow, it tore her belly,
> it cut through her insides, splitting the heart.
> Having thus subdued her, he extinguished her life.
> He cast down her carcass to stand upon it.[27]

Marduk cleaves her in two and fashions heaven from one part of her body, and the earth from the other. Afterwards, he decides to create man, and the gods determine that one of their number must die so that this can come about:

> 'It was Kingu who contrived the uprising
> and made Tiamat rebel, and joined battle.'
> They bound him, holding him before Ea.
> They imposed on him his guilt and severed his blood (vessels).
> Out of his blood they fashioned mankind.
> He (i.e., Ea) imposed the service and let free the gods.[28]

Finally, the myth recounts how Marduk establishes the worlds of gods and men, respectively, and how the gods construct the heavenly dwelling for Marduk which is to serve as a model for the earthly temple, and how the details of its worship are ordered. Supplementary texts inform us that the battle of the *Akitu* festival was dramatically performed by two groups of participants, whose battle

> not only commemorated the primordial conflict between Marduk and Tiamat; it repeated, it actualized, the cosmogony, the passage from chaos to cosmos. The mythical event was present:

'May he continue to conquer Tiamat and shorten her days!' the celebrant exclaimed. The combat, the victory, and the Creation took place *at that very moment*.[29]

There seem to have been several different elements to the *Akitu* festival in its original form. The supplementary texts also indicate that, prior to his victory, Marduk was 'imprisoned' in the kingdom of death, that is, he was at the mercy of the forces of chaos. This characteristic is probably the result of some aspects of the Sumerian-Babylonian fertility god Tammuz having been transferred to the figure of Marduk. Tammuz is a typical fertility god, who personifies nature; when vegetation withers during the dry season, it is understood as Tammuz' descent to the underworld, and when rain and fertility return to the land Tammuz is seen as arising from the dead. This is yet again a creation motif. Drought represents chaos, which dominates the created world for a period of time, but the forces of the cosmos triumph through the figure of Tammuz; when he breaks the chains of death, chaos is subjugated. The cosmos is created anew.[30]

There are other elements in the *Akitu* festival which may be subsumed under the category of creation. For example, on the eighth and eleventh days of the festival an 'assignment of fate' takes place; this means that the gods determine the events of the year to come. In a manner of speaking, the new year itself, with all its occurrences, is created. Myth and cult contribute to ensure that the year's 'fate' will be fortunate, in that the evil god Kingu originally received the tablets of fortune from the hands of Tiamat, and gained power over the destiny of the world; but Marduk, after Kingu has been killed, takes over the tablets and thereby becomes the one who ensures fertility and good fortune for the new year.[31]

Another element of the *Akitu* festival that points in the same direction is the performance of the *hieros gamos*, the sacred marriage, which is an archetype of men's and women's sexual relations with each other; it can be seen as an aetiology of the institution of marriage in the primeval era. But when Marduk and his consort, who in the cultic act were surely represented by the king and either a queen or high priestess, perform sexual intercourse, they create fertility for the new year. This conception is very common in agricultural societies, and fits quite naturally into the context of the New Year Festival.[32]

Our review of the Babylonian New Year Festival indicates that it contains a number of the myth types we identified above: theogonic, cosmogonic, cosmological, and anthropological elements of myth are prominent. Similarly, the 'cult myth', i.e., the narratives of the foundation of the temple and its worship, are present, as are nature myths, underworld myths, and others.

One could hardly ask for a better text than *Enuma Elish* to illustrate how close are the connections between the myth itself, the idea of creation, and the New Year Festival. It is furthermore evident that the battle motif plays a significant part in the myths of the festival, since the primary acts of creation emerge from the battle with and triumph over the evil powers. At the same time it is clear that the maintenance of the cosmos is established through repeated victory over the threatening power of chaos.

This dualistic aspect of the creation myth is everywhere present, and can also be observed in a complex of myths which is in many ways a connecting link between the myths of Babylon and Israel, namely the myths from Canaanite Ugarit (Ras Shamra) in Syria; of these more will be said below.

At this point we should mention that there are many creation myths in which battle is not the backdrop of the creation; instead, we meet some primeval beings who give birth to the gods, who in turn later create the world, man, and so forth. This conception was combined in *Enuma Elish*, as we saw, with the battle motif in such a way that the gods are said to be born to the primeval beings Tiamat and Apsu, whereas the creation of the world and man emerged from the results of the battle. The Greek Orphic myth of the creation relates that in the beginning there was only time; from this were formed the ether and chaos, in which arose an egg which, hatching out, produced the gods and the world. In this story the birth motif is altered in a more abstract sense; the creation occurs as a sort of emanation.[33]

The Ba'al myth in Ugarit

Canaanite religion, which we have come to know through the discoveries of texts at Ras Shamra-Ugarit, has not bequeathed us an actual creation myth. The supreme god, El, is named more or less *en passant* as 'creator of the created', 'father of the gods', 'father of man', or as 'father of years', that is, as the god who creates time and is lord of its passage. His act of creation is thus not described more closely.

But some of the Ugaritic myths contain traces of a battle reminiscent of the one we observed in *Enuma Elish*. However, it is not El

who leads the fray, but the Ugaritic fertility god Ba'al who ultimately defeats the divinity Yam. In one passage the latter seems to
be identical with the dragon Lotan (Leviathan in the OT), a sea
monster with seven heads. Yam, however, is otherwise designated
the 'sea prince' and therefore corresponds to the sea goddess Tiamat
in the Babylonian epic. It is obvious that the myth signifies that
Ba'al represents the cosmos, which he establishes against the incur-
sions of the god of chaos, Yam. In the words of Johannes Pedersen:

> It happened in the primeval era and happens in the cult through
> the battle of the god of life with the dragon, to prevent him
> from seizing power. We find resonances of this theme in the
> magnificent description of Yahweh's work of creation in the
> book of Job (ch. 38).

Pedersen seems thus to feel that the battle motif is a fragment of a
greater epic of creation.[34]

It is in any case another conflict that dominates the myths from
Ugarit: the struggle between Ba'al and Mot, the god of death. The
texts are difficult of access, but in 1938 the Danish scholar Flemming
Hvidberg published his pioneering analysis, later translated into
English under the title *Weeping and Laughter in the Old Testament*; it
deals primarily with the texts pertaining to the battle between Ba'al
and Mot. Hvidberg succeeded in arranging the sequence of the texts
so that their dramatic tension becomes plain; the work seems to
have been performed at the Autumn Festival in which, after the dry
season, it was essential to secure rain and renewed fertility.[35]

The drama seems to begin when Mot taunts Ba'al through his
herald, and threatens:

> I shall assuredly pierce thee!

After a sizable lacuna we hear what conditions on earth will be like
after Mot has succeeded in banishing Ba'al to the underworld:

> When Ba'al enters his [the earth's] interior,
> when he goes down into his mouth,
> then the olive tree will assuredly be burnt off,
> the crop of the soil and the fruit of the trees.

Ba'al, who refuses to be intimidated, sends word to Mot,

> Depart, tell the gods' son Mot,
> repeat it to Il's beloved one, *ġzr*:
> A message from Aliyn Ba'al,

words from *Aliy qrdm*:
'A shame on thee, gods' son Mot!
Am I thy slave and thy serf?'

There are again large lacunae in the text, but in any event Ba'al is later ordered to descend into the earth with his retinue:

And thou, take thou thy clouds, thy wind,
thy water spout, thy rain;
with thee thy seven attendants,
thy eight wild boars.
. . . .
'Thou art to be counted among those descended into the earth,
and thou art to know nothingness,
for thou wilt be doomed.'
Aliy[n] Ba'al obeyed.

But before he descends to the underworld Ba'al performs the important act of copulating with the goddess in the form of a heifer, thus preserving future fertility:

He loved the heifer in [the land] of the plague,
the cow in the field of the strand of death.
He lay with it seven and seventy (times),
it was mounted (?) eight and eighty (times),
it conceived and gave birth to *mt*.

Ba'al's descent to the underworld provokes the gods to sorrow; even El climbs down from his throne, sits down on the ground, casts dust upon his head, rends his clothes, and says:

'Ba'al is dead.
What will become of Dagān's[36] son's people?
What will become of the hosts belonging to Ba'al?
I will descend into the earth!'

However, it is not El, but Ba'al's sister and consort, 'Anat, who descends into the underworld in search of Ba'al. She finds him and, while she laments and 'gorges herself on tears, drinks tears like wine', the sun goddess Shapash comes up to her:

Loudly she cries to the torch-bearer of the gods, Šapš,
'Do load Aliyn Ba'al upon me.'
The torch-bearer of the gods, Šapš, obeyed,
she raised Aliyn Ba'al on to 'Anat's shoulder.
When she had placed him (there),
she carried him up to Ṣapān's peak.

She lamented him and buried him,
laying him in the cave of the gods in the earth.

Afterwards she brings several hundred animals as sacrificial offerings for Ba'al. Another god ascends Ba'al's throne, but 'Anat's love for him is undiminished.

Like the co[w's] heart for its calf,
Like the shee[p's] heart for its lamb,
So 'Ana[t's] heart is for Ba'al.

'Anat visits Mot, demands that he release Ba'al from his clutches, and when she has at length described how all vegetation withers under the rule of Mot, she takes up arms against him. An interesting feature of their combat is that Mot is not merely regarded as the representative of death and drought; he also represents that which characterizes nature in the dry season, the ripened grain. 'Anat deals with him accordingly:

With the sword she clove him,
with the riddle she winnowed him,
in the fire she burnt him,
between the two millstones she ground him,
in the field she sowed him
in order that the birds might eat his remains.

The transition occurs with 'Anat's victory over Mot. Ba'al's resurrection is assured; the sorrow of the supreme god, El, gives way to joy:

'Heaven rains fatness,
and the wadies flow with honey.
Then I know that Aliyn Ba'al has revived,
that the Zbl Ba'al of the earth exists.'
. . . .
Ltpn Il Dpid rejoiced,
he placed his feet on the footstool,
he opened his mouth wide and laughed,
he lifted up his voice, crying,
'I will sit down to rest,
and my soul reposes in my breast;
for Aliyn Ba'al has revived,
the Zbl Ba'al of the earth exists!'

A fragment has been preserved which depicts the decisive battle between Ba'al and Mot:

> They look at each other like two burning coals,
> Mot is strong, Ba'al is strong,
> they gore like wild bulls,
> Mot is strong, Ba'al is strong,
> they bite like snakes,
> Mot is strong, Ba'al is strong,
> they pull like fiery (steeds),
> Mot fell, Ba'al fell on him.
> Šapš calls to Mot,
> 'Do listen, Oh gods' son Mot,
> how darest thou wrestle with Aliyn Ba'al,
> how should not thy father Ṭr Il hear thee?
> He will assuredly pull the props of thy seat,
> he will assuredly overthrow the throne of thy kingdom,
> he will assuredly break the sceptre of thy judgeship!'

Mot is frightened and acknowledges Ba'al's right to his throne. Another group of texts relate how Ba'al constructs a temple with a trapdoor which represents the fissure in the clouds through which rain comes. Ba'al seats himself upon his throne and says:

> 'I alone am the one who is King of the gods.
> Indeed, who fattens the gods and the humans,
> who sates the hosts of the earth.'

The centre of gravity of this myth is different from that of the Babylonian myth of creation; and yet the basic motif is identical: the world of man is secured by the performance of the cultic acts with which the myth is connected. Just as Marduk's victory over Tiamat establishes the created earth, so Ba'al's triumph over Mot preserves fertility. These stories present two sides of the same question; in both cases the actual subject is the basis for human existence. Incidentally, the two myths have quite a few things in common; we should assign the differences to their respective cultural backgrounds.

The sort of myth we find at Ugarit is first and foremost the type Heiler calls a nature or vegetation myth, which is common to many agricultural societies. In this kind of cult,

> the rhythm of life is acted out, as it expresses itself among people whose life is dependent upon the annual renewal of nature through the autumnal rains and the subsequent revival of all vegetation which had been extinguished by the barren heat of summer. When in the cult sanctuary the gods recapitulate in concentrated form these fundamental events, culmi-

nating in the victory of the god of life, they create that life which will come to flourish in the coming year.[37]

These cultures are vividly aware that the poles of existence are life and death and that life can only be attained through the battle against death. At the same time they acknowledge that death is the ultimate destiny of man, and they even know that life is begotten out of death.

The nourishing grain sprouts from the earth, where the dead belong. Therefore Mot can be identified with the grain, since it is through his body that it is procured and made useful for man.[38]

The ancient Canaanites were familiar with the truth to which the Gospel of John bears witness, 'Unless a grain of wheat falls into the earth and dies, it remains alone; but if it dies, it bears much fruit' (John 12.24).

In what has preceded, we have attempted to define myth. We have noted that it is through myth that the religious instinct finds the means of self-expression. Only through myth can primitive man, who thinks in religious terms, give form to his understanding of the most elemental and profound problems of life. Further, it is only through myth that he is intellectually able to comprehend the nature of the things that surround him. Did the Israelite think in the same way? Did he also have to seek recourse to myth when he wished to express himself religiously? To this question we must now turn.

2

THE USE OF MYTH IN GENESIS

Benedikt Otzen

Primeval history and mythology

Fernando Arrabal, the dramatist of the absurd, is reported to have said: 'I find it curious that death and religion do not constitute the major theme of all poetry; but then, when you get right down to it, they really do!' If by the word 'death' we understand the limiting term of the human condition, and if by 'religion' we understand man's relationship to the 'powers' which determine his existence, then we must admit that the Old Testament lives up to Arrabal's specifications. To put it another way, the OT expresses the Israelites' self-understanding. The reader of the OT receives a richly varied impression of the way the Israelite understood his existence, his relationship to the world around him, and his relationship to Yahweh, the God of Israel.

However, it is important for us to realize that all this is concealed behind an account of Israel's 'history', which for the Israelite meant a narrative of Yahweh's dealings with his people. The OT is Israel's account of her own history; this definition is in fact applicable to the entire work: every expression in the OT is based on a conception of Yahweh as the God who works in and through history. Moreover, this is true even if we are talking about the Psalms, the Wisdom literature, or whatever else could be cited as textual examples which seem to depict timeless religious insights in a more abstract fashion.[1]

The question is whether this assertion also applies to the subject of our study, the book of Genesis. It is often somewhat schematically asserted that Gen.1–11 is largely myth, while 12–50 consists of patriarchal sagas within which a separate section is formed by the Joseph story, an edificatory *Novelle* or short story.

We shall later have occasion to observe that the distinction between myth and saga is quite fluid in the OT and it would perhaps be more appropriate to emphasize the thematic differences that separate these two sections of Genesis: the primeval history of chapters 1–11 aims at a cosmic and universalistic perspective. It speaks of the origin of all mankind, and of how the first men destroyed their relationship to the Creator God, Yahweh; in brief, it tells us how sin came into the world. The remainder of Genesis focuses on a much narrower spectrum. Here the principals are Israel's ancestors, the patriarchs Abraham, Isaac, and Jacob, together with Jacob's sons, from whom the twelve tribes are said to be derived. The centre of gravity of these accounts lies in the situations in which Yahweh chooses the patriarchs to become the forbears of his people, Israel, promises them the land, assures them of progeny 'as the stars of heaven, and as the sand which is on the seashore', and in return merely demands that Israel acknowledge him as her God. Again in brief, the patriarchal stories explain how the blessing came upon Israel.[2]

At all events, it is in the primeval history that we have to look, if we want to discover myths; the question is whether we shall find myths in the sense we defined in the previous chapter, where we suggested that myth speaks of events which take place outside historical time and space; and additionally, that myth is related in one way or another to cultic proceedings. We should admit at once that it is difficult to give an unambiguous reply to this question, since in the case of the OT matters are nowhere as straightforward as is the case with the myths of Mesopotamia and Canaan. The difficulty is occasioned by the fact that the Genesis accounts, in particular those of the so-called 'priestly' stratum, represent a late deposit of tradition which received its final form only in the post-exilic period. For the time being, however, it will be sufficient to note that the Genesis narratives are myth-like, and that they undoubtedly reflect an old Israelite mythological tradition.

Even Geo Widengren, who has ordinarily a keener nose for mythical elements in the OT than most, says of the mythical materials in the primeval history that they are largely based upon epic traditions; or, in other words, that we have them only in reworked form. Widengren maintains that it is especially in the poetical sections of the OT that the myths have been preserved in a purer, less reworked form (see the following chapter). This is hardly accidental, since the poetical sections are most closely linked to the cult; in fact in many cases it is possible to regard them, at least in their original form, as cultic texts.

Widengren also points out that we have in the OT only a remnant of the national literature of ancient Israel; and that this remnant of which we have the final version has been censored and structured in accordance with the ideas of the circles who, in post-exilic Israel, had the responsibility for this final retouching. It is therefore striking, in view of these considerations, that so many mythological materials are still preserved in the OT, a fact which persuades us to recognize that there must have been a powerful mythical tradition in old Israel. It is even conceivable that there once existed 'a now lost Hebrew epic literature of a mythical content'.[3]

Gerhard von Rad offers a quite different opinion of the myths of Genesis. He maintains that the expressions of mythical origin, which we meet in Gen. 1–11, are separated from any mythological context and have in Israel long been made into cosmological stereotypes which were part of the indispensable stock of priestly learning.[4] Further, K. I. Johannesen, a young Norwegian scholar, proposes completely to dispense with the use of the word 'myth' in connection with the narratives of Genesis; he maintains that

> the presuppositions of mythopoesis were not really present within the framework of Israelite Yahwism. . . . Moreover, the belief in Yahweh as the only real God of Israel was a factor most unfavourable to the assimilation or the fresh production of myths. Myths prefer to involve several gods. . . . Myths lack their essential framework in Israel.[5]

The German scholar Werner H. Schmidt offers a more sophisticated view of the matter; he is convinced that Israel did not originally have a story of Yahweh as Creator; it was only after the entry into Palestine and as a result of the influence of the surrounding religions that Yahweh came eventually to be understood as a Creator God: 'Israel shared her mythical conceptions of the beginning of the world with the rest of the ancient Orient, and derived them from that source.' However, Schmidt adds, Israel fashioned her own belief in creation in the course of a continual struggle with these mythical conceptions. He holds that the Israelite was not concerned with the ability of myth to explain how the world and man came into being, but only with the fact that it was Yahweh who had created both. Thus Schmidt asserts that Israel was able to formulate her belief in creation only by means of mythical expressions, but he concludes that, 'where the myth forced its way into the credo, it became transformed, transfigured, or even subjugated', to such a degree that in reality it ceased to be myth at all.[6]

This much is true: the narratives in the opening chapters of Genesis do not have the character of real myths. The texts cannot be set, like the Mesopotamian and Canaanite texts, in direct relation to the cult. As Johannes Pedersen says, 'The real old myths which the Israelites must have had have not been preserved to us.'[7] Nonetheless, we contend that the accounts in the first chapters are based on old Israelite myths, since it is possible to point to other passages in the OT which contain fragments of myths which must originally have stood in a much closer relation to the cult. These fragments are able to tell us a great deal about the ideas which must once have characterized the Israelite consciousness. Above all, these ideas are found in the OT Psalms, which are indirect evidence that what we have called the myths of Gen. 1–11 do in fact represent an actual layer of mythological thought in the OT. Moreover, we shall attempt to show that these 'myths' reflect a cultic reality which held a central place in Israel's religious life.

The following chapter will illustrate the roles which were played by the idea of creation and the creation myth in the OT Psalms, and will also try to indicate how recent research, taking its point of departure in the Psalms, has succeeded in demonstrating that the ancient Israelites celebrated a New Year Festival in which the concept of Yahweh's battle with the life-destroying powers and his victory and concomitant confirmation of the cosmic orders enjoyed a prominent place.

For the time being it will suffice if we note that there are texts other than Gen. 1–11 which show that the Israelites must have thought in mythological categories when they attempted to describe the world in which they lived. In the introductory chapter we observed that the notion of creation occupies a central position in real myth; it is accordingly only natural that, confronted with Genesis, we should turn to the creation narratives and examine their relationship to the mythical.

The Priestly Work and the first creation narrative

Everyone who has ever worked with the OT knows that there are two creation narratives, each distinct in its own way from the other, in the beginning of Genesis. The first account begins in ch. 1 and continues three or four verses into ch. 2; the other begins at ch. 2.4 and is in what follows tightly linked to the stories of paradise and the fall. The very fact that there are two versions is interesting in itself; it suggests that when the various versions of the OT came under redaction it was felt that the two narratives supplemented each other in a useful way. There must, then, have been elements in one narrative which would have been welcome in the other.

It is consequently important that we should attempt to penetrate to the fundamental differences between the two narratives. However, we should not attach too much significance to the more striking but superficial differences, such as the varying sequences of the works of creation, the different descriptions of conditions prior to the creation, and so forth; rather, we must try to find out what it is that essentially distinguishes these accounts from each other.

The first narrative represents a priestly tradition; even if this story contains a number of very ancient elements, it is in its present form not a popular narrative but an expression of learned speculation about the beginning of things.

Earlier research used to maintain that the Pentateuch was composed of at least four different sources, the Yahwistic, Elohistic, Deuteronomic, and Priestly, of which the first was often dated as early as the epoch of David, while the last was assigned to a period after the Babylonian exile. These different, originally independent sources or documents, were supposed to have been woven together to form the present Pentateuch. Moreover, it was thought possible to trace these sources in the historical writings all the way up to the books of the Kings.

The Deuteronomic source (D) was held to begin with the book from which it has taken its name, and to continue in the connective passages of Joshua, Judges, I and II Samuel, and I and II Kings. The Elohistic source (E) was thought to begin at Gen. 15 and to be visible only sporadically thereafter (the classic E-narrative concerns the sacrifice of Isaac in Gen. 22). As far as Gen. 1–11 is concerned, it was held possible only to find traces of the Yahwistic (J) and the Priestly (P) sources; by way of anticipation, we should remark that the first creation narrative was traditionally assigned to P, and the second to J.

Nowadays we are hardly so assertive in questions concerning the redaction of the Pentateuch. Instead of independent sources, scholars prefer to speak of strata of tradition, and instead of the assumption that the sources were combined by a process of literary redaction, it is now assumed that in the course of time the various accounts were 'narrated together'.[8]

Regardless of how one looks at these matters, no one today would deny that there are in the Pentateuch, besides a quantity of indisputably older narratives, i.e. those which have above all been assigned to the tradition stratum J, also a number of sections sharing a common imprint, and which apparently derive from priestly circles. These sections may be comprehensively termed a source or better, a tradition stratum; it was added in connection with the final redaction of the Pentateuch during the centuries after the Babylonian captivity.

The 'priestly' aspect of these sections is most apparent in their interest in the law, and especially in cultic regulations. They also have a somewhat 'erudite' character: various traditions have been assembled so as to form a chronological system which is especially visible in the monotonously repetitive genealogies which the reader of the Bible often ignores (the descendants of Adam in Gen. 5, the descendants of the sons of Noah in ch. 10; cf. the latter half of ch. 11). If we compare the two creation narratives with these characteristic priestly genealogies, we quickly sense that in the first creation account we are in the arid atmosphere of the priestly scriptorium. The first account of the creation bears to a certain extent the same characteristics as the genealogies, and it is not accidental that the priestly technical term for the genealogies, *tōlᵉdōt* ('book of genealogy'), is used of the first creation narrative. This occurs in the short concluding phrase in 2.4a, 'This is the genealogy of heaven and earth'.

Thus the first creation narrative is probably best understood as a summary of the course of the creation, plus an account of the world order which results from the creation. It has also been suggested that the God we encounter in the first creation narrative is more a God who brings order to things than one who actually creates. He separates from each other things that do not belong together and transfers them to their correct positions. The verb 'to create' (*bārā'*; 1.1, 21, 27; 2.3) is certainly significant, but there is another Hebrew verb that occurs frequently throughout the chapter, and which is characteristic both of the priestly linguistic tone and of the priestly view of creation. This is the verb-form *hibdīl*, which should be translated 'to make division', 'to part', or 'to separate from each other'. Thus light and darkness are separated from each other (1.4); the firmament of heaven separates the waters above from the waters below (1.6f.), and the sun and moon separate day from night (1.14–18). *Hibdīl* is a true priestly word; it occurs frequently in priestly legislation, which stresses the importance of separating the clean from the unclean, and the sacred from the profane. It serves in such contexts to impose order or create system, so that things which do not belong together will not get mixed up.[9] The identical impulse to create system and order is present in the efforts to undertake botanical and zoological classifications of the plants and animals 'according to their own kinds' (vv. 12, 21, 24, 25). Here too the important aspect is not that of 'scientific' systematization but of the priestly concern 'to separate' clean from unclean genera.

The priestly views are most obviously present in the distribution of the various elements of the creation over a period of six days, so that the entire scheme is crowned by the institution of the sabbath (ch. 2.2–3). This clearly represents an attempt by the priesthood to legitimate the important sacral institution which enjoyed such great significance in later Judaism by tracing its inception back to the creation itself. The sabbath first received the prominent position in Judaism, which it has retained until our times, during the period of the Babylonian captivity. And the fact that it was not until postexilic times that the priesthood felt it necessary to give this sacred custom so unshakable a foundation agrees well with the common opinion that the priestly source or priestly redaction of the Pentateuch must belong to this late date; as it does also with the opinion that the first creation narrative must have received its final touches in this period.

Now the question is, what happens to the mythical dimension when it has been accommodated to this system of dry, priestly erudition? Is not von Rad right when he asserts that the only traces of mythical concepts we perhaps still can discern have become fixed as 'cosmological keywords'? And Werner H. Schmidt is surely correct in affirming that the Israelite did not compose an account of the creation to tell us *how* the world came into being, but to assure us of the fact that it was Israel's God who did it, and to tell us about his intentions in imposing order on the world.

At least as far as the first creation narrative is concerned, it is probably not unlikely that its final, 'priestly' elaboration was carried out in the manner suggested by von Rad and Schmidt. However, it is important to recognize that the priests thereby made use of mythological concepts which, at least at some early point in their history, must have had currency in the Israelite consciousness. The priestly account of the creation represents an *interpretation* of traditional material, and it is clearly a legitimate procedure to attempt to penetrate this interpretation in an effort to discover the older sphere of ideas.[10]

In past attempts to distinguish between the oldest tradition and the later priestly retouching of it, scholars have often tried to divide the text into an 'action narrative' ('God did such and such') and a 'verbal narrative' ('God said . . . and then he said', etc.). One can undertake a literary critical analysis, as was common in earlier research, and thereby assume that the unification of the two narrative types occurred as a strictly literary process. Or one can assume that the joining together of the various traditions took place during a stage of oral transmission, which means that the process was one of gradual assimilation of traditions to each other over a shorter or longer period of time. In both cases the result would be that the priestly narrative is primarily discernible in the 'verbal narrative'. In late Judaism Yahweh has become the distant and elevated divinity who creates by means of his word alone. The more primitive and more mythological understanding is to be found in the 'action narrative', in which God 'makes' things.

Werner H. Schmidt has recently undertaken a very thorough analysis of ch. 1. He concludes that after the priestly elements have been peeled away from the whole, we are left with an older, characteristically more mythological account of the creation which presumably never existed as an independent literary entity, but which contains the elements we should in all probability regard as the oldest strata in a long process of transmission. If we isolate these elements, we arive at the following juxtaposition:

2: And the earth was waste and void, and there was darkness over the great deep. And the spirit of God hovered over the waters.

4: And God separated the light from the darkness.

7: God made the firmament and separated the waters beneath the firmament from the waters above the firmament.

9 (according to the Greek translation): And the waters under heaven gathered themselves into one meeting-place, and the mainland became visible.

12: The earth brought forth green herbs, which yielded seed . . . and trees which yielded fruit with seeds.

16: God made the two great lights, the greater to rule by day, and the lesser to rule by night, and the stars; and God placed them in the firmament of heaven.

21: And God created the great sea animals, and the whole swarm of living creatures, with which the waters swarm . . . and all winged creatures.

25: And God made the wild animals . . . the cattle . . . and all of the creeping things of the earth.

26–27: Then God said: Let us make men in our image, so

they will resemble us, to rule over the fish of the sea and the birds of heaven, the cattle, and all the wild animals on earth, and every creeping thing that creeps upon the earth. And God created man in his image; in the image of God he created him.
2.2: And God rested (?).[11]

Of course, such a division of the text should be accepted only with the greatest of reservations, but there can hardly be any doubt that most of the elements Schmidt has removed belong to the priestly redaction. To take but one example: the scheme of seven days, which because of the sabbath came to characterize the final form of the chapter, can now clearly be seen to be secondary, since there are more than six works of creation. There are in fact eight, a difficulty which the priestly redaction was only able to overcome by positioning two of the works of creation (the separation of sea and land and the generation of plants) together on the third day, and two other works (the creation of the animals and that of man) on the sixth day.[12]

Thus we approach the problem of the mythical elements in the text. Scholars have at the end of the day not reached general agreement on the question whether the scheme of seven days was a product of the priestly redaction. One must admit the possibility that already at an early point in the development of the creation narrative the creation was distributed over a certain number of days, which the priests merely modified in order to accommodate their special understanding of the sabbath. The Swiss scholar Paul Humbert attempted in 1935 to demonstrate that the seven days scheme was original to the narrative, and that it pointed to a dramatic performance of each of the units of creation, one to each of the seven days of the old Israelite New Year's Festival.[13] If correct, this suggestion would imply that the creation narrative of Gen. 1 was originally a cultic dramatic text, which would in turn suggest, on the basis of the definition of myth we proposed above, that the narrative represented a real myth. Humbert points to the fact that the Babylonian creation epic *Enuma Elish* (discussed above) was read aloud on a number of the days of the Babylonian New Year Festival. In this connection, Humbert reminds us that the post-exilic Festival of Booths, which represents a partial reworking of the pre-exilic New Year Festival, spanned a period of exactly seven days.

Helmer Ringgren, the Swedish scholar, feels that this parallel with the seven days of the Festival of Booths must be treated with respect; he is nevertheless critical of Humbert's attempt to interpret Gen. 1 as a specifically cultic text. Ringgren agrees that there is a substratum of cultic myth beneath the text, but he holds that in its present form it has been so much refashioned, among other things in polemic against the cult of Canaan, that it would be incorrect to term it a cult text.[14]

The representation of chaos in Genesis

It is difficult to know where to begin in order to come to grips with the cultic myths which underlie the text in question. Let us turn to Gen. 1.2, which reads as follows, according to the RSV:

> The earth was without form and void,
> and darkness was upon the face of the deep;
> and the Spirit of God was moving over the face of the waters.

This single verse has been the subject of endless discussion. What does it really mean? Is it a true description of chaos, that is, a depiction of powers inimical to Yahweh, who ruled before Yahweh had established cosmos? Alternatively, is the verse trying to describe created matter in its original formlessness; that is, does it depict an intermediate state, between nothingness and created matter, but within the framework of creation? Von Rad is an adherent of the latter point of view, not least because he conceives of v. 1 as standing in isolation, i.e., as a sentence which describes an unconditional beginning which temporally precedes all that follows.

It is, however, not at all clear that we should so understand the text. In another article Paul Humbert argued from purely grammatical principles that v. 1 is a temporal subordinate clause, v. 2 a descriptive addition, and v. 3 the main sentence. Following him and Eduard Nielsen we should translate the three verses as follows:

> When God began to create heaven and earth – the earth was then waste and void, and there was darkness upon the deep, but a storm of God lashed upon the surface of the waters – then God said, 'Let there be light', and there was light.[15]

This translation makes the relation to other oriental creation narratives more evident. Scholars have previously observed that a strikingly large number of accounts of the creation begin with a sort of subordinate clause which usually tells us what did not exist before the creation took place, or they describe conditions at the very beginning of the process of creation. Thus *Enuma Elish* (the words signify ('When on high') begins,

When on high the heaven had not been named,
firm ground below had not been called by name,
naught but primordial Apsu, their begetter,
(and) Mummu-Tiamat, she who bore them all,
their waters commingling as a single body;
no reed hut had been matted, no marsh land had appeared,
when no gods whatever had been brought into being,
uncalled by name, their destinies undetermined –
then it was that the gods were formed within them.

What follows is a list of the first gods, and the plot advances
afterwards towards the conflict which eventually culminates in the
battle between Tiamat and Marduk discussed above.[16] Other frag-
mentarily preserved creation narratives, including a very ancient
one from Sumer, contain introductory formulae which in a similar
fashion have the aspect of a temporal clause. The following example
is taken from a ritual text which was employed in the exorcism of
demons during temple restoration:

When Anu had created the heavens,
(and) Nudimmud had built the Apsu, his dwelling,
Ea nipped off clay in the Apsu;
he created Kulla for the restoration of [the temples].[17]

These similarities between the biblical and extra-biblical creation
narratives may only imply that such temporal formulae were an
element in tradition, a tradition which has thus been preserved in
the late moulding of the priestly creation account. On the other
hand, the similarities are not without importance. If we translate
Gen. 1.1–3 as we have done above, the description of the chaos
state in v. 2 takes on greater significance.

Few would deny that elements of a description of chaos are
present in v.2; the question is, are they significant? It is possible
that these expressions were intended by the priestly redactor(s) to
highlight the message of v.1 that it is God who has created everything. These expressions can therefore be understood as emphasizing the aspect of creation as dynamic activity on God's part.[18] By
the same token, it is important to recognize that these concepts
must have spoken to their audience; they must in some sense have
represented reality to them. We know that this was in fact the case
from the aforementioned descriptions in the Psalms of Yahweh's
battles with the powers of chaos in his efforts both to create and to
establish his creation. These descriptions will be discussed in the
next chapter; here it is sufficient to observe that it would be difficult

to develop a feeling for the mythological background of the creation narratives in Genesis without such passages as Pss. 89.9–12 and 74.12–17.

'The earth was then waste and void'; the distinctive Hebrew expression *tōhū wā–bōhū* does not denote 'the non-existent', since the Israelites were not given to this sort of abstraction. It is composed of two elements of which the first, *tōhū*, is often used to characterize the desert, which to the Israelite represented the unusable, the empty, that which lacks all substance in reality and scarcely belongs to the ordered world of man. At the same time the desert connotes something threatening to the Israelite. If the desert expands, the cultivated world must give way and collapse. Thus the word *tōhū* bears with it associations of a danger which threatens human existence.[19]

If *tōhū* is thus associated with the desert, the other element, *bōhū*, seems to keep company with darkness. The Phoenician goddess of the night, *Baau*, is mentioned in later Greek texts, and it is conceivable that there is some connection between her name and the Hebrew word, a connection which would by reason of its origins suggest that the Hebrew word had some mythological connotations. However, the connection of *bōhū* with the Canaanite-Phoenician religious background is uncertain. The decisive thing is to note that in order to describe the chaos state which preceded creation the redactor chose expressions suggestive of the frightening and ominous. This certainly applies also to darkness. In the well-ordered world there is a regular cycle of day and night; light proves day after day that it is able to banish darkness. Constant darkness suggested to the Israelite not only something frightening, but dangerous as well. Darkness is above all a characteristic of the kingdom of death; thus, while darkness rules, evil powers, who are messengers of death, have an easy time of it. Light, on the contrary, is associated with life, peace, blessing, justice, and truth.[20] Darkness has no qualities of its own, but rather expresses the absence of light and its correlatives; it is therefore a characteristic of situations or areas in which human life can not endure.

Again, the expression, 'the deep' or 'the cosmic deep' seems to be to a high degree endowed with mythological content. The Hebrew word is *tᵉhōm*, and although the etymology has been disputed, we assert that it has a purely linguistic connection with the name of Tiamat in Babylonian mythology. Moreover, as we saw in our discussion above (cf. pp. 13ff.), Tiamat is identical with the sea.

As we shall see in connection with the flood narrative, *t^ehōm* signified to the Israelite a threatening potential for annihilation; the word has a demonic ring to it in many contexts, but is generally strongly' depersonalized. In the hymnic passages which describe Yahweh's battle with the sea, the designation *t^ehōm* is regularly replaced by the designations 'Leviathan', 'Rahab', or 'the dragon', which represent the demonic and rebellious capacities of the sea. But *t^ehōm* is also possessed of a certain ambivalence in Israelite thinking: on one hand it suggests the threatening and destructive torrents, on the other the life-giving waters which ensure fertility. We shall return to this double aspect of Israelite feeling about water later.

If we compare Eduard Nielsen's translation of Gen. 1.2 offered above (cf. pp. 31f.) with that on which both RSV and AV are more or less agreed, one striking difference is immediately apparent. The well known expression, 'the Spirit of God moved upon (RSV, was moving over the face of) the waters' is here translated, 'a storm of God lashed upon the surface of the waters' (NEB reads, 'a mighty wind that swept over the surface of the waters'). The very fact that the Hebrew text allows of two so radically different readings shows that there are difficulties in the text. The major conclusions of the various attempts to interpret this passage are as follows.

1. The traditional rendering ('the Spirit of God moved upon the face of the waters') has been taken to signify that the passage itself was positioned in antithesis to the preceding words: in spite of the fact that in the beginning the world was unformed, God is here seen as reigning even over the state of chaos; God's spirit is present 'as an expression of both God's will and preparedness to act', and this was intended to suggest 'that even before the first work of creation the world was subordinate to God and dependent on him'.[21]

2. Hermann Gunkel understood the passage quite differently as an anticipation of the act of creation. Finding some support in a number of other Semitic languages, he translated the verb *rāḥaf* in the sense of 'brood', rather than 'hover' (AV and RSV translate the verb to mean 'move', perhaps in order to avoid strange associations). He held that we have here to do with a faint reminiscence of the concept of the 'world egg', familiar to us from other religions. The implication is that the world originates like a bird which is hatched out of the liquid contents of the egg. The concept is supposed to have been known to the Phoenicians, although it is admittedly attested only by very late Greek sources.[22]

3. A third understanding comes closer to our proposed transla-

tion, and likewise expresses the conviction that the passage belongs to the phase of creation. It has been pointed out that the Greek translation of the OT reproduces the unclear Hebrew verb *rāḥaf* by a verb which means something like 'to attack' or perhaps 'to inflict'. If we bear this in mind and also recall that the Hebrew noun *rūaḥ* signifies both 'spirit' and 'wind/storm', it would be reasonable to translate the phrase in question to mean 'but the storm of God attacked the surface of the sea' (lit. 'face of the sea'). Interesting in this rendering is of course the fact that a battle-motif emerges with which we are familiar both from the Babylonian creation epic and from the OT Psalms. There is also an implied connection, as Eduard Nielsen has remarked, with the flood in Gen. 8.1, 'God made a wind blow over the earth, and the waters subsided . . . ', and there is also a link with the account of the crossing of the Red Sea in Ex. 14.21. The weakness of this position, of course, lies in the uncertainty of the translation of the verb.[23]

4. The fourth possibility too is beset with difficulties. The principal difference between this and the other interpretations can be expressed as follows: the three views discussed above all assume that the phrase, 'but the Spirit (wind/storm) of God . . . ' represents an antithesis to the preceding passage, so that the act of creation in a manner of speaking begins with this phrase. However, there is reason to consider, not least because of the verb's participial form, whether one should not translate as follows: 'and a storm of God moved back and forth over the surface of the waters.' The first difficulty this translation encounters has again to do with the peculiar verb *rāḥaf*. It occurs otherwise only twice in the OT, once in Deut. 32.11, which refers to the flying back and forth of an eagle over its nest (which is filled with young); and Jer. 23.9, in which the prophet depicts his spiritual breakdown in a sentence that should be translated, 'all my bones are moving this way and that'.[24]

Now the expression *rūaḥ 'elōhīm*, besides meaning 'Spirit of God' and 'storm of God', can also mean 'violent storm'. In a number of places in the OT the divine names *'ēl* and *'elōhīm* are used simply to express a superlative (e.g. Gen. 23.6; 30.8; Ex. 9.28; I Sam. 14.15; Jonah 3.3, etc.).[25] (RSV usually translates 'mighty' or 'very great'; cf. the colloquial use of 'almighty', which is really a divine epithet, in modern English.) The translation of Gen. 1.2 suggested here implies that the state of chaos which preceded creation was also characterized by a mighty storm. According to late Greek accounts, the Phoenicians believed that the creation resulted from a meeting between the wind god Kolpia and his consort Baau, the goddess of the night, to whom we referred earlier in connection with the word *bōhū*. On the other hand, other Phoenician accounts represent creation as coming forth from water and darkness.[26]

Yahweh and chaos

In the preceding sections we have several times referred to Johannes Pedersen's *Israel*; in the brilliant concluding chapter of the first volume of this work, entitled 'The World of Life and Death', the author sketches out what he feels essentially comprised the Israelite's picture of his world. The created and ordered world in which man lived was surrounded by what Pedersen calls the three 'non-lands' of the desert, the deep (*tᵉhōm*), and the kingdom of death (*šᵉ'ōl*). All three of these areas are, according to Pedersen, hostile to life and characterized by the sovereignty of darkness, which as we noted earlier, was understood as the negation of life-giving light. In the author's own words:

> The Israelitic conception of the universe is an expression of the conflict between life and death, or, rather, the fight for life against death. The land of life lies in the centre, on all hands surrounded by the land of death. The wilderness lies outside, the realm of death and the ocean below, and these send in their tentacles from all sides and make of the world a mixture of life and death, light and darkness. But life *must* be the stronger. The great terror of the Israelite is that some day evil shall get the upper hand, and chaos come to prevail in the world of man. The important thing is to have sufficient blessing to be able to keep evil at bay.[27]

With these observations in mind, it is easy to see that the concepts we met in the second verse of the first creation narrative all have reference to the three 'non-lands' described above; taken together they comprise a picture of what to the Israelite was chaos, the opposite of the well-ordered world, the cosmos. We have also observed that many of these concepts have, or had at one time, some form of mythological content. Then what distinguishes the concept of chaos we encounter in the first creation narrative of the OT from the representations of chaos which we know from the religions of Israel's neighbours?

Common to all of these various traditions is the idea that chaos still threatens the world of man, despite the fact that it was originally

defeated, or perhaps tamed, at the creation. The desert may force
its way into good arable land and make it uninhabitable by man;
death may 'ease his tentacles' into human existence in the forms of
illness and sin, which can wreck man's existence; and death itself
is the final reality to which every man is subject. Moreover, at any
moment the primordial sea, which lies beneath the earth and above
the firmament of heaven, may break through and annihilate the
cosmos, as in fact happens in the story of the flood.[28]

To the later prophets it was a certainty that breach of covenant
on Israel's part could mean the dissolution of the cosmos and a
return to chaos. The following passage from Jeremiah is characteristic of this point of view; he imagines what will become of Israel,
if the people do not repent, and his visionary account makes full
use of the notions of chaos which we have seen in the creation
narrative (Jer. 4.23–26):

> I looked on the earth, and see, it was waste and void *(tōhū wā-
> bōhū)*;
> and to the heavens, their light was gone;
> I looked on the mountains, and see, they were quaking,
> and all the hills trembled back and forth;
> I looked, and see, there were no men,
> and all the birds of heaven were flown;
> I looked, and see, the orchard was a desert,
> and all its cities were laid waste
> before Yahweh, before his searing wrath.[29]

The distinctive difference between the idea of chaos in Gen. 1
and the similar conceptions we know from related cultures is probably that according to the Israelite view chaos is unable to produce
cosmos, which is a regular feature of the other systems of creation.
Thus in Babylonian religion it was the chaos beings Apsu and
Tiamat who produced the first gods, and the body of Tiamat from
which heaven and earth were constructed at the creation. In the
Phoenician tradition, as we noted above, it was the meeting of either
wind and darkness or of the deep and darkness which was the origin
of 'all things'. According to the Egyptians, who possessed several
cosmogonies, the deep and darkness also figured at the creation.
The Israelite may sometimes understand chaos as something
actively hostile to God; this is obviously the point of those passages
which speak of God's battle against chaos. But the idea of creation
is nevertheless – or perhaps for precisely this reason – more radically
worked out in the priestly creation narrative: Yahweh alone is the
sovereign Creator. Chaos is inactive; it produces nothing, nor does

it in reality offer Yahweh any opposition. That is to say that in this account Yahweh is not compelled, as in the Psalms, to do battle with chaos; rather, chaos is portrayed as something passive, as a state of affairs which can be characterized as a negation of the creation of which Yahweh is author.

For this reason the first creation narrative is distinguished by the ruling idea (discussed above) that at the creation God *orders* things; he positions the elements of chaos in their places in relation to the created and ordered world: the deep above the firmament of heaven and beneath the earth, and 'in one gathering-place, which he called the seas'. Darkness is similarly limited to the hours of night, the 'waste and void' desert is given a place outside the world of men, and so on. The motif of battle has been suppressed; chaos is a thing God can command after his own good pleasure.

There is therefore an unexplained element in the Israelite view of chaos. On one hand, the mythological, virtually dualistic idea makes itself felt, that chaos is a real power over against Yahweh, one with which he is forced to do battle and, repeatedly, to subjugate. On the other hand it is quite obvious that the idea, which is not confined to the priestly creation narrative, is that Yahweh is the sovereign ruler who uses chaos as his willing tool. This thought is visible in the flood narrative, and also in the prophetic descriptions of the state of annihilation which Yahweh will bring about when he comes to punish his recalcitrant people. It is thoroughly typical of the OT that we find this tension between a mythological and a more reflectively theological view of things side by side.

The thought of Yahweh as sovereign is expressed a number of ways in Gen.1; the use of the verb *bādal*, 'to separate', is discussed above; it is most distinctive that *bārā'*, 'to create', is a word reserved exclusively for the description of divine creation. As in the case of the verb *bādal* the specifically priestly understanding of things is made manifest by the choice of this word; also, the fact that it is used repeatedly in conjunction with the ordinary verb which means 'to make or do' (e.g. vv. 7, 16, 25, 26, 31) supports our opinion related above that the narrative is composed of several strata. Finally, the priestly disposition of the elements of the text crops up in the form of the strong emphasis on the *word* as the means of God's creative activity (also discussed above). The concept of the word as the only link between the Creator and his creation establishes an objective distance which is intended to prohibit any attempt to understand the creation as a part of God's being; it is solely a product of his will.[30] Thus the priestly circles strive in a number of ways to prevent a mythological understanding of their account of creation, which is nevertheless composed from older mythological materials and doubtless in an older form was moulded by mythological conceptions.

It will of course be impossible for us in these pages to analyse the whole of the priestly creation narrative. Nevertheless, we should perhaps mention a couple of passages in which we can again sense the efforts of the priestly craftsmen to suppress a mythological idea and thus prevent the hearers from wandering onto paths of thought which, according to the priestly point of view, lay uncomfortably close to paganism. It is also likely that these conceptions were much too close to those of Israelite 'popular religion'.

In this connection, it is usual to point to the fact that in vv. 11f. God does not himself create the green plants, but commands the earth to bring them forth. It is conceivable that the background of this passage is the ancient mythological idea of the 'Earth Mother' who 'gives birth' to the products of the soil. On the other hand, it is equally possible that the verses represent a veiled polemic against, among other things, the Canaanite identification of the fertility god Ba'al with all plant life. To prevent such an identification, it is possible that the redactors here decided to interpose the earth as a mean term between the Creator God and the vegetable world.

A similar polemical thrust seems to be present in v. 21, in which God creates the great sea beasts. The Hebrew word *tannīn* is employed in several of the by now much discussed poetic representations in the OT of Yahweh's battle with the chaos monster. The monster is often called Rahab or Leviathan (see above, p. 34), but in Ps. 74.13, Isa. 27.1 and Isa. 51.9 the subject at issue is Yahweh's slaying of 'the dragon', *tannīn* (in the first cited text it occurs in plural form). It would appear that the priestly redactors have only scant enthusiasm for these more mythologically flavoured descriptions of the chaos battle, since in Genesis they maintain unequivocally that the 'dragons' are a part of God's work of creation, are obedient to him, and thus cannot be his opponents.[31]

The second creation narrative

While the attempt to form a clear understanding of the position of myth in the first creation narrative offers some difficulties, as we have seen, we would expect matters to be less ambiguous in the second, which includes the stories of paradise and the fall (Gen. 2.4b–3.24).

The second creation narrative does not belong to the priestly source. From its use of the divine name Yahweh, this narrative is traditionally assigned to the source or stratum of tradition known as the Yahwistic; in any event, it received its final form at an earlier period than did the priestly account, and contains old materials which have been considerably less reworked than is the case with the other stratum. The mythological features of J (as this narrative is designated) have not been forced so much into the background, but are visible on the surface of the narrative.

The general perspective of the first creation narrative was cosmic. It dealt with the Creator God's arrangement of the entire world system, and its centre of gravity lay in the relationship of God to the world, or, in other terms, in the relationship of chaos to cosmos. By contrast, the field of view is distinctly narrower in the second creation narrative. Here the subjects are primarily man's relationship to God and man's relationship to the world in which he lives. Again distinctive is the fact that while the first account speaks of 'heaven and earth', the second prefers the phrase 'earth and heaven', and moreover, heaven is only mentioned on this one occasion (Gen. 2.4), and does not appear subsequently. It seems as if the polar opposition of chaos and cosmos has in the latter narrative been reduced to the dialectic of the uncultivated, waterless wasteland, and the 'human world', the world in which man is able to live. This relationship is evidenced by the play on words which characterizes ch.2, *'ādām* (man) and *ᵃdāmāh* (arable land); man seems to be related to the land in some way, and is in fact created from it. On the other hand, the arable earth is dependent on man's cultivation of it (cf. vv. 5,15).[32]

Not only do the two narratives have different foci and intentions; it is clear that each has also its own particular cultural background. In the first account, as we have seen, water (represented as the 'deep', *tᵉhōm*) conveys associations of malevolence and danger; it is only when God has tamed it and shown it to its place in things that it becomes useful to man. The connection between Tiamat and *tᵉhōm*, plus a number of other considerations, make it probable that the foundations of this conception are Babylonian. After all, it was primarily in the inundations of Mesopotamia that water demonstrated an inherent demoniacal quality. By contrast, in the second account drought is the major threat to human existence; water is there regarded solely as life-conferring, and even as the most important necessity for the cultivation of land so that human life can endure. This characteristic naturally corresponds to the conditions of the Syro-Palestinian area, and seems to have had influence on the second creation account.

Thus the description of 'chaos' and of creation has a different character in ch. 2; it is in a sense more primitive, perhaps even more naive, than the first. It makes no attempt to depict a primeval cosmic situation with threatening and sinister characteristics; instead, it is content to list the various absent requisites which are necessary in order to make the earth inhabitable to man, to make it an *ʾadāmāh* on which *ʾādām* can dwell: there were no trees or shrubs, no plants in the fields, since Yahweh had not yet allowed the rain to fall. And moreover, it is added in an amusing sentence: there weren't any men to cultivate the land! Here, cosmos is not a concept of cosmic dimensions, but rather a simple and in an extraordinarily literal sense, earthy concept. Cosmos is that world which man creates through his labours, and with the help of the rain which is sent by a gracious God. The world picture here described is not the work of learned priestly speculation. Rather, its origin is to be assigned to the Palestinian farmer's feelings of community with the earth he cultivates.

None of the above should be taken to signify, however, that there are no suggestions of the influence of cultures external to Israel in this narrative. In the first place, we can again observe the characteristic indication to which we called attention in connection with the first creation narrative; namely, that the description is introduced by a temporal clause, as also occurs in the Babylonian narratives of creation (see above, p. 32). Other things also point to the Babylonian ambit. In the citation from *Enuma Elish* quoted above (p. 32) was a sentence which describes conditions before the creation in a manner similar to that of Gen. 2.4ff.; it mentions the fact that the basic necessities for human activity were then lacking: ' . . . no reed hut had been matted, no marsh land had appeared . . .'

The same notion is more clearly expressed in a creation text that was found in the ruins of ancient Sippar, somewhat to the north of the city of Babylon:

> A holy house, a house of the gods in a holy place, had not been made;
> a reed had not come forth, a tree had not been created;
> a brick had not been laid, a brick mould had not been built;
> a house had not been made, a city had not been built;
> a city had not been made, a living creature had not been placed (therein);

Nippur had not been made, Ekur had not been built;
Uruk had not been made, Eanna had not been built;
the Apsu had not been made, Eridu had not been built;
a holy house, a house of the gods, its dwelling, had not been
   made;
all the lands were sea;
the spring which is in the sea was a water pipe;
then Eridu was made, Esagila was built –
Esagila whose foundations Lugaldukuga laid within the
Apsu –
Babylon was made, Esagila was completed.[33]

If the verse about the spring in the sea has been correctly translated (there are admittedly some problems in it), it would seem to
be reminiscent of Gen. 2.6, in which the act of creation is introduced
by the eruption of a 'spring', which waters the earth. The AV here
recommends 'mist' rather than 'spring', which the RSV admits as
a variant; however, the Hebrew word probably signifies subter-
ranean waters which well up to the surface. Of greater significance
is the fact that several Babylonian creation narratives, in agreement
with Gen. 2, maintain that man was created to cultivate the earth,
and by this means to sustain the cosmos. While it is true that the
Babylonian texts usually also affirm that man was created to serve
the gods by the ministrations of the cult and the offering of sacrifices,
it is clear that to be able to attain these goals men must maintain
the irrigation system, cultivate plants, breed cattle, and so forth.[34]

In other words, there are a number of connective links between
Gen. 2 and the Babylonian tradition. This becomes even more
evident when we consider the description of man's creation in Gen.
2 (man in v. 7; woman in vv. 21–24). In the priestly narrative in
Gen. 1 the account of the creation of man is quite colourless. In
part the diction is affected by theological problematic (e.g., 'in our
image, so they will resemble us'), which for reasons of space we
cannot examine more closely; in part also, the account is characterized by rather dry, almost juridical language (e.g. 'male and
female' etc., instead of 'man and woman'). By way of contrast, in
Gen. 2 the creation of man occupies the centre of the stage; this
creation is, as we noted above, practically a precondition of the
establishment of the rest of the work of creation. Whereas in Gen.
1 the creation of man is represented as the summit of the divine
work, in Gen. 2 it is the basis.

The idea of how man is created is taken straight over from Israel's
neighbours. Egyptian paintings show us how the god Khnum

fashioned man from clay on a potter's wheel, and the verb which in Gen. 2.7 is used of the creation of man usually designates the activity of the potter (*yāṣar*). Further, according to an Egyptian text, 'man is clay and straw, and the god is his builder'.[35] Side by side with the notion we meet in *Enuma Elish*, according to which man was formed from the blood of the rebel god Kingu, we find in other Babylonian texts the idea that man was fashioned out of clay. In the words of the epic of Gilgamesh:

> Aruru washed her hands,
> pinched off clay and cast it on the steppe,
> [on the step]pe she created valiant Enkidu.[36]

In the text we cited earlier (p. 32) which deals with the creation of Kulla, the god of bricks, and other gods of clay, the passage concludes:

> He created the king, for the mainten[ance of the temples];
> [he created] mankind for the doi[ng of the service of the gods(?)].[37]

Alexander Heidel offers a still more interesting text in his *Babylonian Genesis*; it dates from the period of Hammurabi, that is, from the first half of the second millennium, and, although it is poorly preserved, it clearly bears witness to a creation tradition according to which man is held to be composed of a mixture of clay and the blood of murdered gods:

> Let them slay a god,
> and let the gods. . .
> with his flesh and his blood
> let Ninhursag mix clay.
> God and man
> . . . united (?) in the clay.[38]

During the second century BC, a priest of Marduk by the name of Berossus wrote in Greek an account of ancient Babylonian religion, an account that has been preserved only in extracts. Berossus tells us that at the creation of man one of the gods cut his own head off at the command of Marduk, after which the other gods mixed his gushing blood with earth and formed man from the resulting compound. 'On this account', Berossus adds, 'they are rational and partake of divine understanding.'[39]

This conception approaches that which we observe in Gen. 2: man is not merely formed out of clay; he also participates in the

divine. In the biblical account this idea is expressed by the suggestion of God's blowing the divine breath of life into man. In ch. 1,
man's special relationship to the rest of creation is implied by the
concept of the 'likeness of God'; in Gen. 2 this relationship is
depicted by the image of man as the recipient of the breath of life
from Yahweh. Thus man became what the RSV calls 'a living
being'. Literally translated, the Hebrew text reads: 'and man
became a living soul' (the same expression is used in Gen. 1 of
animals). The tension hereby indicated is not the later Greek distinction between soul and body, but, as is often acknowledged
nowadays, that between body and life. Anyone is able to see for
himself that life departs from the body together with breath, which
thus may be taken to represent the life principle. However, this
expression should not be over-interpreted; the notion that man's
breath is blown into him by Yahweh is not identical with Berossus'
description of the Babylonian concept that at creation man receives
the blood of a god and is accordingly equipped with 'divine understanding'. Rather, the biblical understanding is that the life of man
is a gift from God, and that when man dies Yahweh takes back the
breath of life.

All the same, the narrative in Gen. 2 accords to man a special
place in relation to the rest of creation. His task in the garden of
Eden is to 'till and keep it', and it is also man who is permitted to
give the animals names, a task which in ancient oriental thought
signified that man was to endow the animals with their various
qualities, corresponding to their names. When man calls an animal
'lion', he thereby gives it 'lion character'. Man thus is included in
the work of creation and regarded as king over it; this is a mythological characteristic with which we are familiar from other cultures:
the first man is perceived as a king, while subsequent kings are,
conversely, understood as incarnations of the first man.[40] In Mesopotamia, the king was occasionally regarded as a living representative of the mythological gardener of paradise.

If, however, man stands in this relation to the rest of creation,
there is nothing to prevent some men from taking precedence before
others. In the conclusion of Gen. 2 we read of the creation of
woman, where the fact that was regarded as self-evident by ancient
orientals, that woman was inferior and subordinate to man, is
expressed in the myth of woman's construction from a rib taken out
of the man's side. This myth has also a positive aspect, since it
attempts to motivate the close relationship between man and

woman, as well as to emphasize that woman's relation to man is in principle different from that of the animals.

Moreover, the sexual element is clearly present in this passage. Some scholars have wondered whether or not the rib is to be understood as a phallic symbol; others think, however, that the rib was chosen because of a Sumerian word-play on the expression 'the woman, who created life', and the word for 'rib'. All this is uncertain. The section is primarily an aetiology, whose sociological intention is to explain and support the ordinarily recognized institution of marriage. We should note in passing that in the history of religions it is quite unusual for the creation of woman to be narrated independently: often this passage is cited with so remote a parallel as that of the Eskimoes; they assert that woman was created from man's thumb.

Paradise and the fall

At this point it would be appropriate to stop and enquire: Just what is the position of myth in the opening chapters of Genesis? We have been able to single out fragments of myth for observation, as well as allusions to myths, but we do not have myths as such in this part of the OT. It appears that Israel adopted a great deal, perhaps even most, of this material from neighbouring cultures, but it is equally clear that the Israelites subjected these materials at every point to a thorough revision.

In short, the Israelite behaved in a sovereign fashion towards the mythical material that he imported. He employed it in his theological speculations about the world order (above all in the Priestly Work), and he used it to work out an anthropology, a view of man, his position over against God, and his position in the world in which he lived. This is especially true of the creation narrative in Gen. 2.

As we have already noted, the second narrative is interested to a far lesser extent than the first in the 'cosmic system'. In spite of what might appear to an outside observer to be its somewhat more primitive character, it attempts above all to develop an Israelite 'view of man'. That this is its goal becomes immediately clear in ch. 3, which deals with the fall. The Yahwistic narrative of creation should probably best be understood as an introduction to ch. 3, since it is first there that significant things are said about the Israelite view of man. Briefly, Gen. 3 tells us how man becomes alienated from God, is driven out of paradise, is prevented from achieving eternal life, and is condemned to an existence in which he is subjected to those terms which are the conditions of ordinary human life.

It should hardly surprise us that someone felt compelled to use myth in speaking of these important events. It is, however, interesting to note that the whole section is composed in an entirely independent way; there are no obvious debts to the works of any other culture. Perhaps the most likely candidates would be the two famous Babylonian narratives, the epic of Gilgamesh and the myth of Adapa; both feature semi-divine figures who almost attain to eternal life, but are at the last moment denied this privilege, which is reserved for the gods.[41] The basic problem held in common by these two Babylonian poems would seem to correspond to at least one of the themes of Gen. 3, the question why all men must die. The Israelite answer to this question, however, diverges sharply from the others; there is no suggestion in the Babylonian narratives that man has acted rebelliously against the Creator God, that is, that he has fallen through sin.

There are, on the other hand, at least some characteristics in the biblical story that point to an external tradition. Should we initially enquire why it is a serpent that plays such a nefarious part in the story, we are struck by the fact that in the epic of Gilgamesh it is a serpent that steals the magical herb which enables the one who eats it to live for ever, and which is called 'Man Becomes Young in Old Age'. In the epic, Gilgamesh is in possession of the plant and is on his way back to Uruk when

> Gilgamesh saw a well whose water was cool.
> He went down into it to bathe in the water.
> A serpent snuffed the fragrance of the plant;
> it came up [from the water] and carried off the plant.
> Going back it shed [its] slough.
> Thereupon Gilgamesh sits down and weeps,
> the tears running down over his face.[42]

Yet the parallelism to which we have called attention does not explain why the serpent behaves as it does. Von Rad has attempted to explain the matter by reference to man's common and natural aversion to snakes, whereas Gunkel avers that the Israelites must have been familiar with some form of demon in the form of a serpent. We would instead suggest that it is necessary to look deeper into the mythological strata of tradition, if we are to understand the serpent's special position here. Either it represents the chaos monster Leviathan, that is, Tiamat, in which case the underlying idea is that the chaos power that was subdued at the creation now begins to make new inroads against Yahweh's authority;[43] or, as Hvidberg has suggested, the serpent represents the Canaanite god Ba'al, who was often iconographically represented in serpent form.[44] If either of these suppositions should prove correct, or if they both should do so, we have here yet another example in which a group of mythological conceptions has been revised by Israelite hands in an entirely independent way.

There are other details in the biblical story of the fall which suggest some sort of connection with Mesopotamia. The idea of a 'tree of life' whose fruit endows the one who consumes it with immortality, is scarcely an Israelite invention. The epic of Gilgamesh, as we mentioned above, features a plant which confers eternal life, and in the myth of Adapa, the hero is at least offered something edible. It is a common characteristic of many oriental mythologies that the tree of life grows in a paradisal garden inhabited by the gods, and that they retain their immortality by eating its fruit. It is also a common idea that eternal life is a divine prerogative; thus even demigods like Gilgamesh and Adapa are prohibited from attaining immortality. The groundwork of this idea is:

> When the gods created mankind,
> death for mankind they set aside,
> life in their own hands retaining.[45]

But is this quite the same conception we find in Gen. 3? The question is difficult and has been much debated. Gen. 2.9 mentions *two* trees, the 'tree of life' and the 'tree of knowledge of good and evil . The latter does not occur in any other known religion, and scholars have wondered whether the original version of the story did not in fact refer to only one tree, the tree of life, whereas the tree of knowledge has been added later.

This could conceivably be the truth of the matter, but the most important thing is to understand the narrative in its final form. In Gen. 2.16f., Yahweh says to Adam, 'You may freely eat of every tree of the garden; but of the tree of the knowledge of good and evil you shall not eat, for in the day that you eat of it you shall die.' In Gen. 3, Adam and Eve eat the fruit of the tree and acknowledge their nakedness. After he has pronounced his punishment upon the serpent and the two humans, Yahweh declares, 'Behold, the man has become like one of us, knowing good and evil; and now, lest he put forth his hand and take also of the tree of life, and eat, and live for ever . . . ', whereupon Adam and Eve are driven out to the east of the garden of Eden.

It is evident that in comparison with the Babylonian stories a middle term has been introduced into the Israelite narrative which at least at first glance obscures its meaning. The parallel would have been obvious if the biblical story had merely said that Yahweh had forbidden Adam and Eve to eat from the tree of life, which was reserved for him alone; that some way or other they attempted to breach the divine command and were accordingly banished, so that they should not be able to procure immortality for themselves. But then, why does the narrative insist that they should not eat of the tree of knowledge? Moreover, why is it that Yahweh begins to take precautions against their eating from the tree of life, which was not even included in the prohibition of Gen. 2.16f., which expressly states that they may eat of every tree except the tree of knowledge?

We could direct vast numbers of questions to this particular text, and the answers would be legion. The 'tree of life' part is in itself comparatively simple; the text declares without more ado that he who eats from it will 'live for ever' (Gen. 3.22). This corresponds to the 'tree of life' in Babylon. But what does this 'knowledge of good and evil' consist of, that one is supposed to obtain by eating the fruit of the second tree? Most readers would probably assume that it signifies ethical knowledge, so that its attainment by man would entail the ability to determine for himself what things should be regarded as good and evil. This would make man autonomous; it would liberate him from Yahweh's authority. Others feel that the expression 'good and evil' posits a pair of opposites as parameters which delimit an entity. In this sense the expressions 'young and old', 'rich and poor', and 'high and low', merely denote the concept 'all' . Thus 'good and evil' could be taken to mean 'all' or 'everything', and in the context of the biblical narrative this would imply that man attempted to rival the gods by achieving omniscience.

Yet another group maintains that the Hebrew expression 'good and evil' does not signify an abstract ethical concept; they hold instead that it is a functional idea which could best be rendered 'helpful and harmful' – to man himself. Thus, according to our narrative, man would be seen as attempting to achieve what a German scholar has termed *Daseinsmeisterung*, the ability to manage one's own existence. This suggestion is not appreciably different from the idea of man's struggling to obtain his own autonomy.[46]

There is, however, a single important aspect of the text which other scholars have observed, and which is not done justice by the

analyses presented above. This is the observation that sexual motifs
enjoy a prominent place throughout the entire narrative. There are
so many of them that they simply must be significant: the serpent,
which was a Canaanite sexual symbol; the two humans' acknow-
ledgement of their nakedness, and their accompanying feelings of
shame; the fig leaves; the curse upon the woman (Gen. 3.16) which
is aimed at the sexual plane; the naming of Eve, which plays on her
maternity; and finally the garment given to both Adam and Eve. It
could be parenthetically mentioned that the fig leaves are hardly a
symbol of chastity, but rather the reverse; it has been observed that
in several ancient cultures the fig was thought to increase man's
sexual prowess; scholars have also considered whether it is not
implicit in the story that the 'tree of knowledge' is a fig tree. It was
in any event a late non-biblical tradition that proposed the apple.

Gunkel was the first in this century to pay attention to these
motifs, but he hardly gave them the weight they deserve. He held
that the story emphasizes sexual awareness and shame as an arche-
typal example of the fact that in his disobedience man abandons
the childlike, unmediated relationship with Yahweh, and becomes
mature and reflective in his relations with him. Gerhard von Rad
takes a slightly different tack when he affirms that the shame is the
most primal expression of the feeling of guilt.[47] The Swedish scholar
Ivan Engnell has dedicated an entire article to the solution of this
problem; in it, in addition to analysing the above-mentioned sexual
motifs, he examines the expression 'to know good and evil', which
in his opinion also has an unmistakably sexual content. The verb
'to know' is often used in the OT of sexual relations, as, for example,
at the beginning of Gen. 4. Engnell further points to two passages
in the OT in which he feels the expression 'to know good and evil'
means 'to have sexual capability'. These are Deut. 1.39, where it is
said of children that they do not know good or evil; and II Sam.
19.35, where the ancient Barzillai is described as one who does not
know good or evil.[48]

If it is correct that the secret of the tree of knowledge is that it
endows the one who partakes of its fruit with sexual capability and
procreativeness – and there is a good deal to be said for this view
– we are immediately impelled to enquire why the acquisition of
this capability should be regarded as a fall from grace. The Israelite
is otherwise known to have had a relaxed view of sexuality *per se*;
he was no ascetic. Engnell replies that the story of the garden of
Eden presupposes that as long as the two humans dwelt in the
garden, they must have enjoyed free access to the tree of life, and

were thus immortal, like the gods. This presupposition explains why the tree of life does not lie under the divine interdict of Gen. 2.16f.; instead, these verses announce somewhat ominously concerning the tree of knowledge, 'in the day that you eat of it you shall die'. This must therefore have meant, according to Engnell: 'If you eat from the tree of knowledge you will in future be denied access to the tree of life, and thereby lose the immortality which you so far have maintained by eating its fruit.'

The question is, of course, why so severe a punishment should be meted out for consuming the fruit of the tree of knowledge. Presumably, the immortality of which Adam and Eve were in possession was what Engnell prefers to term 'individual' immortality. Thus the meaning of the narrative should be that the original plan called for only the two humans to live together with Yahweh in the garden of God for eternity. However, when by eating from the tree of knowledge they acquired the ability, similar to Yahweh's, to *create new life*, they became able to create an eternal line of successors. According to the primitive cast of thought, the tribal ancestor lives on through his descendants; thus in Genesis Adam and Eve are seen as achieving yet another form of immortality besides that of the individual, namely so to speak a collective immortality. In so doing, they have made themselves equal to God.

Yahweh's reaction is immediate; in Gen. 3.22 he says 'The man has become like one of us, knowing good and evil; and now he shall not put forth his hand and take also of the tree of life, and eat, and live for ever.' As Engnell has argued, this sentence must mean: man shall *no longer* have access to the tree of life so as to *retain* his personal immortality.[49] This reading makes the curse upon Adam in Gen. 3.17–19 appear to be completely logical, for there death is established after the fall as the ultimate condition of man. Man has encroached upon a divine right and in return is compelled to surrender his earlier privilege.

Myth and the Israelite view of man

The Israelite account of the first man and woman in the garden of Eden and their relationship to the Deity is more profound than the parallel Babylonian narratives. Both the epic of Gilgamesh and the myth of Adapa seem rather to play with the notion that man might be able to attain immortality, only subsequently to recoil from it; some ugly vicissitude of fortune seems to snatch eternal life out of the hands of these heroes. Myths of this type were used in the OT to say something of great significance about the relationship between God and man; however, this is only one side of the Israelite view of man. Furthermore, Gen. 3 says something about the human condition in the world in which men live; this is sketched out in Yahweh's addresses to the serpent, Adam and Eve after the fall (Gen. 3.14–19).

The most conspicuous aspect of these verses is the abundance of aetiologies contained in them. They offer explanations of an extensive list of aspects of the world of man: the serpent's isolated position among the other animals; its strange method of locomotion; its food, which is said to be the dust of the desert; the mutual enmity between man and serpent; the travail of woman in pregnancy and birth; her inferior position in respect of her husband; man's struggle to wrest food from the earth; the reality of death and the burial custom; the interpretation of Eve's name and the origin of clothing. But even these are not the most important elements in this passage.

To our way of thinking, it is of greater interest to enquire whether there are mythological survivals in this section. Superficially, this does not seem to be the case, but we should like to assert that these verses are indeed characterized by mythological conceptions. In the preceding sections of this chapter, we have repeatedly succeeded in detecting reminiscences and fragments of myths and mythological ideas in the opening chapters of Genesis, many of which display numerous strong links with the mythology of Babylon. However, we have also pointed to the fact that these conceptions have been so comprehensively reworked within the biblical tradition, and with such independence and assurance, that we can almost speak of a form of 'demythologizing'. Now, it is not certain that we shall be able to get a grip on the mythological qualities of these verses merely by stressing their observable mythological motifs, since it is conceivable that the mythological nucleus lies concealed beneath the surface.

Thoughts along these lines have been propounded by James Barr, who holds that if we should wish to understand the relationship of the OT to myth and its use of myth, then it is most important that we should attempt first to discover the 'total world-view' of myth. Barr suggests that this view is delineated by the correspondences or harmonies between the divine and the human, between gods and nature, between the primeval era and the historical present, and so on. Now, Barr shows that 'in Israel the correspondence pattern of mythology was broken', mainly as a result of the special Israelite understanding of history.[50] This is an important point to which we shall return. But of equal importance is the question whether the 'total world-view' of myth, one way or another, has left its stamp on the Israelite understanding of man and world. Not so much in terms of 'correspondences' or 'harmonies', but rather in terms of the opposites 'chaos' and 'cosmos'.

What is the nature of the total world-view that underlies the entire complex of ideas about creation in the primeval era and cultic re-creation in the historical present, which in the introductory chapter of this work we have claimed are central to all true myths? It is the idea that the world and man are located in *a field of tension between chaos and cosmos*. This is the universal perception of the world and human existence which myth expresses. It is, so to speak, the theme of myth. And however the individual Israelite and the OT otherwise relate to myth, the OT is permeated at all levels by this total world-view, just as the Israelite's conception of his existence is determined by this theme. As Pedersen says in the passage already cited, 'The Israelitic conception of the universe is an expression of the conflict between life and death. . .'[51]

This total world-view is evident in the curses pronounced by Yahweh upon the serpent, Eve and Adam after the fall; here the mythological theme constitutes the basis of an Israelite anthropology. The main idea is that at the creation Yahweh originally subjugated the power of chaos, referred it to its place in the scheme of things, and established limits to its ability to make itself felt. After the fall it is man's lot in life to lead an insecure existence in a threatened world, that is, to live in tension between that which sustains (Yahweh's power to preserve the integrity of the cosmos) and that which menaces (chaos, which it is in Yahweh's power to unleash).[52] We shall see how this ruling idea is framed in Gen. 3.14–19.

Verses 14 and 15 are addressed to the serpent; the many aetiologies contained in this section are discussed above. However, the speech which ordains eternal enmity between man and serpent is more than a mere reference to or explanation of existing conditions. If it is correct, as we previously affirmed (cf. p.47), that the serpent figure was chosen as the seducer in the Genesis narrative because it is identical with the dragon Leviathan, which in turn represents the great deep, *tᵉhōm*, and if we combine this insight with the fact that in Genesis the serpent appears in connection with the desert, a most interesting implication arises. Johannes Pedersen was earlier quoted as describing the Israelite's three 'non-lands'; behind the figure of the serpent it is possible to glimpse two of them, the great deep and the desert. Thus we feel that the passage in question refers not merely to man's relationship to the serpents, but to his eternal struggle with the destructive forces of chaos. Von Rad interprets verses 14f. unmythologically, but none the less quite correctly recognizes that they deal with 'man's relation to the evil with which he has become involved'.[53] An element of futility may be discerned in the fact that the battle is unceasing: man will never achieve absolute security.

Thus the curse upon the serpent suggests a provisional definition of the human condition after the fall. Moreover, as we have also seen, the curse upon woman in Gen. 3.16 operates on the sexual plane, in the forms of pain and suffering. It is the third of the 'non-lands' of the Israelite that here reveals its power, the power of death and Sheol which stretch out their threatening tentacles towards the woman in labour. 'He who is struck by evil, by unhappiness, disease, or other trouble *is* in Sheol.'[54] The idea is that chaos – in this case in the form of Sheol – menaces human existence. The tension between cosmos and chaos is here immanent; in the very function in which woman fulfils her (biblically) most distinguished task, that of bringing new life into the world, she is herself threatened by the life-destroying powers.

Just as in the context of the Genesis narrative the curse on woman is connected with one of the two trees in the garden of Eden, namely the tree of knowledge, which endowed her with the ability to produce offspring, the curse upon man is connected with his being driven away from the tree of life. Man is no longer to be nourished at his ease by this tree, but must at great cost win his food from the earth. The idea of the first part of the curse upon man (vv. 17f.) is that his work, and so his existence, are continually threatened by 'thorns and thistles', a recurrent designation in the OT for the vegetation of the desert. Again it is the wilderness, the land of chaos, that threatens to engulf the cultivated arable land which, as we have seen the Jahwistic creation narrative identifies with the ordered world, the cosmos.[55] This is powerfully emphasized: the ground itself is accursed (v. 17), and this points forward to v. 19, where Sheol, the kingdom of death, is assigned the ultimate mastery over human life.

The myth of the flood

As we have previously related, chaos is, according to the OT ideas of creation, more passive than it is in the cosmogonies of the cultures

which surrounded Israel. Yahweh is seen as the sovereign ruler of
chaos; he allots to the forces of chaos their place in the world system
and simultaneously sets limits to their depredations; however, he is
also able to set these forces free when he so chooses. The passages
dealt with in the previous section show that in the world after the
fall chaos is permitted considerably greater latitude than previously
was the case.

This grand conception culminates in the story of the flood, in
which the waters of chaos, *t^ehōm*, are released against mankind (Gen.
6–9). This story attempts above all to illustrate Yahweh's sovereign
power to destroy the world which he himself once created. However,
an element of tension is preserved in this narrative, too, since the
judgement upon the created world is not universal: Noah and his
family are allowed to survive. Further, Yahweh ensures world order
after the flood by means of a promise which may be understood as
a recapitulation of the original creation: he will never again destroy
the world, the course of the year shall be according to law (Gen.
8.21f.), and the laws of nature shall in future have universal validity.
The promise is confirmed by a covenant, of which the objective sign
is the rainbow (Gen. 9.12–17).

The flood narrative has therefore theological significance within
a wider context, while at the same time it describes the Israelite
understanding of the world and of nature. It should not surprise us
to learn that ancient myths were employed here in order to depict
Yahweh's relationship to the created world. The connection
between this narrative and the Sumerian-Babylonian flood myth is
evident, as is the dependence of the former upon the latter. It would
be beyond the purposes of this work to go into this subject in detail.
The Babylonian flood narrative is related in the epic of Gilgamesh,
which recounts how the hero, who is searching for the plant that
confers eternal life, comes at length to Utnapishtim, the only man
who ever 'came along, and found life in the assembly of the gods',
that is, who received divine immortality. In the eleventh tablet of
the epic Utnapishtim relates how he dwelt in Shurippak on the
Euphrates:

> That city was ancient, (as were) the gods within it,
> when their heart led the great gods to produce the flood.

The god Ea, so the story goes, tells Utnapishtim about the god's
plans, and says:

> Tear down (this) house, build a ship!

Give up possessions, seek thou life.
Forswear (worldly) goods and keep the soul alive!
Aboard the ship take thou the seed of all living things.
The ship that thou shalt build,
Her dimensions shall be to measure.
Equal shall be her width and her length.

The following passages circumstantially recount the tale of the construction of the ship in seven days, and how it was loaded with provisions and wealth:

[Whatever I had] I laded upon her:
Whatever I had of silver I laded upon her;
whatever I [had] of gold I laded upon her;
whatever I had of all the living beings I [laded] upon her.
All my family and kin I made go aboard the ship.
The beasts of the field, the wild creatures of the field.
    All the craftsmen I made go aboard.
. . . . .
I watched the appearance of the weather.
The weather was awesome to behold.
I boarded the ship and battened up the entrance.
To batten down the (whole) ship, to Puzur-Amurri, the
    boatman,
I handed over the structure together with its contents.

With the first glow of dawn,
a black cloud rose up from the horizon.

An exhaustive list of gods of storm and misfortune are then named; these give free rein to their powers;

For one day the south-storm [blew],
Gathering speed as it blew, [submerging the mountains],
Overtaking the [people] like a battle.
No one can see his fellow,
Nor can the people be recognized from heaven.
The gods were frightened by the deluge,
And, shrinking back, they ascended to the heaven of Anu.
The gods cowered like dogs
. . . . . Crouched against the outer wall.
Six days and [six] nights
blows the flood wind, as the south-storm sweeps the land.
When the seventh day arrived,
    The flood(-carrying) south-storm subsided in the battle,
which it had fought like an army.
The sea grew quiet, the tempest was still, the flood ceased.

I looked at the weather: stillness had set in,
And all of mankind had returned to clay.
The landscape was as level as a flat roof.
I opened a hatch, and light fell upon my face.
Bowing low, I sat and wept,
Tears running down on my face.
I looked about for coast lines in the expanse of the sea:
In each of fourteen (regions)
　　　There emerged a region(-mountain).
On Mount Nisir the ship came to a halt.
Mount Nisir held the ship fast, allowing no motion.
. . . . .
When the seventh day arrived,
I sent forth and set free a dove.
The dove went forth, but came back;
Since no resting-place for it was visible, she turned round.
Then I sent forth and set free a swallow.
The swallow went forth, but came back;
Since no resting-place for it was visible, she turned round.
Then I sent forth and set free a raven.
The raven went forth and, seeing that the waters had
　　diminished,
He eats, circles, caws, and turns not round.

Utnapishtim accordingly makes a thank-offering, and the gods
swarm 'like flies about the sacrificer'. However, the god Enlil, who
was author of the whole affair, is indignant that a remnant of
mankind has survived, and blurts out, 'Has some living soul
escaped? No man was to survive the destruction!' To this the wise
god Ea replies:

Thou wisest of gods, thou hero,
how couldst thou, unreasoning, bring on the deluge?
On the sinner impose his sin,
　　On the transgressor impose his trangression!
(Yet) be lenient, lest he be cut off,
be patient, lest he be dis[lodged]!
Instead of thy bringing on the deluge,
　　Would that a lion had risen up to diminish mankind!

Enlil allows himself to be persuaded and boards the ship:

Holding me by the hand, he took me aboard.
He took my wife aboard and made (her) kneel by my side.
Standing between us, he touched our foreheads to bless us:
'Hitherto Utnapishtim has been but human.
Henceforth Utnapishtim and his wife shall be like unto us gods.

Utnapishtim shall reside far away, at the mouth of the rivers!'
Thus they took me and made me reside far away,
At the mouth of the rivers.[56]

It is easy to understand why the Israelites could not resist this splendid tale. It should be unnecessary to point out the many astonishing points of agreement between the biblical and Babylonian versions. The oldest Sumerian and Babylonian accounts can be dated as far back as the third and second millennia, which rules out any discussion as to which tradition is dependent on which; the biblical account is clearly derived from the Babylonian.

But yet again we have occasion to emphasize the independence with which the Israelites seem to have dealt with this myth; it has been worked into the theological context already discussed, so that it now relates how man's revolt against his Creator increases, while God remains in possession of his power over creation and knows how to use it. The Babylonian account sadly lacks a similar theological base; the epic of Gilgamesh seems practically to imply that the flood of waters results from an access of divine spleen. 'How couldst thou unreasoning bring on the deluge?', Ea asks of Enlil. The following section offers what is at any rate the germ of an explanation, and is at least preferable to the explanation offered in the parallel version, the epic of Atrahasis, where the gods are said to have sent the flood because men had multiplied so much that their noise disturbed the sleep of the gods.[57]

There is no doubt that from a literary point of view the Gilgamesh epic is far superior to the biblical flood narrative. The Genesis account contains quite a number of unclear and contradictory passages (some refer to one pair of animals, others to seven pairs; the chronological sequence is unclear, and so on). The reasons for this are that the priestly redactor(s) reworked the text on the basis of their own point of view, and, further, that they attempted to compound variant traditions into a unified whole.[58]

There are other sections of Genesis for which there are good reasons for intensive study. The two accounts which now separate the narratives of the fall and the flood (Cain and Abel, Gen. 4; the fragmentary story about the 'sons of God', Gen. 6.1–4) are strongly marked with mythological characteristics. It is perhaps possible to glimpse, far down in the oldest stratum of the narrative of Cain, reminiscences of an ancient ritual murder in which a shepherd was sacrificed to ensure the fertility of the fields.[59] However, the present form of this narrative represents an aetiological tradition intended to explain the origins and peculiarities of the Kenites; moreover, and probably more important, the narrative is to some extent a parallel to the story of the fall, whose sequence of events it mirrors (i.e., crime, examination, curse, expulsion, followed by Yahweh's solicitous care).

The remarkable story about the 'sons of God' who become attracted to the daughters of men, mix blood with them, and so produce the race of giants, is commonly regarded as one of the most mythological texts in the OT. This is probably correct, but we should also note in passing that this fragment too runs parallel to the narrative of the fall. The theme is yet again Promethean: man heedlessly arrogates to himself something of the nature of the gods and is punished for it; moreover, the punishment obviously has something to do with eternal life and death.

Seen in a different perspective, the narrative of the 'sons of God' recalls the story of the Tower of Babel in Gen. 11, which is indubitably an aetiology, but which also has overtones of the Titan motif: man rebels against God (the original point of the story is probably that the men intend to invade the heavens)[60] and is accordingly punished.

Conclusion

In our introductory chapter we delimited the genre of myth in relation to other literary forms: myth speaks of things that occur outside historical time and space, and which only coincide with history during the cultic repetition of the primal event. Saga, in contrast, is rooted in history and gives at least the impression of being a historical narrative. How, then, do the more or less mythologically coloured accounts of the opening chapters of Genesis relate to the sagas further on in the book, and so to actual history? Would it be correct to say that the stories about the first men, the fall, and the flood belong in some sense outside historical time and space? Finally, what of their relationship to the cult?

To take the last problem first: we have previously encountered this question in the form of Humbert's attempt to treat the first creation narrative as a cultic text. At least this much is sure: the idea of creation, the establishment of the created world, and the unleashing of the life-destroying violence of the forces of chaos plays so prominent a part in Israelite cult that the myths which *underlie* the creation and flood narratives without doubt must have enjoyed a central position in the great cultic complex we so comprehensively subsume under the heading of the New Year Festival. In the next chapter a more precise attempt will be made to deal with this problem in connection with the Psalms. Here it would be appropriate to quote Johannes Pedersen on the subject of the New Year Festival:

> Just as the myth of creation, Enuma elish, was recited at Babylon in honour of Marduk who re-created the world at the feast, it seems natural to suppose that the Israelites, when celebrating Yahweh's assumption of power as the creator of the world, recited a myth of creation. The story of the creation given in Gen. 1 conveys the impression of a didactic exposition rather than a cult-myth. Of course it was based on a real myth, but it is highly probable that a myth of creation recited in the temple of Jerusalem had the character of a glorifying account of the work done by Yahweh in primeval ages.

In a similar vein he says of the flood narrative:

> The myth of the deluge, ending with the promise of the regular alternation of the seasons (Gen. 8.22), would fit in well with the autumn festival, all the more so since Noah who is saved from the chaos, reintroduced then, is the first vine grower (Gen. 9.20).[61]

Decisive in this connection, however, is the fact that no matter how these myths were employed in the cult, the Israelite cult was in any event permeated on all levels by what was termed the 'total world-view' of myth, the understanding of existence as determined by the tension between cosmos and chaos. In short, it was the task of the cult to reinforce the cosmos and combat the destructive forces which assail it.

We have many times in the course of this chapter referred to the Israelite's independent attitude to the myths he had borrowed from abroad, and to the fact that he always subjected these materials to revision when he attempted to express his own understanding of the world. If we were to try to explain *why* the Israelite behaved in this way in relation to the mythical, we would quickly arrive at the fundamentally and specifically Israelite nucleus of Israel's religion. The explanation is to be found in the Israelite understanding of God, and in the Israelite view of history. To put it somewhat sharply, we maintain that the Israelite views on God and history brought about a tendency to replace the original, real, cult-bound myth of the primeval era with accounts of the high points of the history of the nation, the events of 'salvation history'. These came to be regarded as the fundamental events of the primeval era, and were accordingly incorporated into the cult and experienced in such a way that they seem gradually to have meshed together with the mythical primeval events. To take but one example: the destruction of the Egyptians at the Red Sea at the exodus is biblically interpreted via the categories of creation and the primeval battle against the chaos monster (see the following chapter, pp. 69ff.). Salvation is identical with creation.[62]

This could be termed a sort of demythologizing, or, conversely, it could be regarded as a mythologizing of history. It is in any case connected with the Israelite's insistence that Yahweh is primarily a God who reveals himself through his activities in history. It is not difficult to grasp the fact that this conception is capable of combination with the idea of creation, since the maintenance both of Israel as a people, and of nature as the necessary presupposition of that people's existence can be viewed as a continuation of the creation. Scholars have described this idea as '*creatio*' and '*creatio continua*', which may be acceptably rendered 'creation and renewal'.[63]

The tendency of mythical and historical events to be approximated to each other is expressed in a remarkable way in the opening chapters of Genesis. It has often been noted that the colourful accounts of creation, flood, and so on are interspersed with a number of genealogies which in a manner of speaking form the skeleton of history. By interweaving these genealogies with the primeval stories the redactors have succeeded in extracting the events of which the latter speak from the world of myth and introducing them into the world of history. Israel's history thus is depicted as beginning with the creation.[64]

The presence of this tendency does not prevent Israel's view of history, as it is expressed in the OT, from also being influenced in a decisive way by the 'total world-view' of myth. The Israelite view of history is characterized by such paired opposites as defeat and restoration, time of woe and time of weal, judgment and salvation; this is most clearly evident in the two collections in which this view of history is most clearly voiced, the works of the prophets and the Deuteronomistic history. When the 'myths' of Genesis are thus stationed at the entrance to Israel's history, they proclaim Yahweh as the Creator of the world, and delineate his relationship to the world and to man. But they also proclaim Yahweh as the one who from time immemorial has shown himself to be the God who can both destroy and rebuild, just as he appears time and again through-

out Israel's history as it is understood in the literature of the Old
Testament.

3

MYTH IN THE PSALMS

Hans Gottlieb

Introduction

In the world of Old Testament scholarship, the Scandinavians are
often characterized as a special group, or 'school'. This character-
ization is both right and wrong. There is no 'school', in the limited
sense that the ideas and opinions of a single authority are uncriti-
cally taken up by his pupils; on the contrary, there is a group of
independent scholars who quite often disagree with one another.
Many of them have received their most seminal impulses from
research which has gone on outside Scandinavia.

With this qualification in mind, we can then proceed to admit
that there is, after all, a sort of school, in the sense of a working
community of individual researchers who take more or less the same
approach to their materials. The members have a number of working hypotheses in common, and in many respects employ the same
methods. The results of this communal effort are most clearly evident in what has been called the 'Scandinavian' understanding of
the Psalms.[1]

Two features are integral to the Scandinavian understanding of
the Psalms. Because of the imprecise use of language which has
crept into critical discussion, both have been described as a 'cultic'
interpretation of the Psalms. We should like to emphasize that it is
important to distinguish between the two senses in which we
actually use the word 'cultic'.

In the first place, the Psalms are not a private devotional work
intended for the individual, even though they may be so used today.
Rather, they are a collection of texts which were once employed in
public worship. These texts were written for, and were first
employed by, the temple in Jerusalem, and they were in use

throughout the period of the Israelite monarchy (ca. 1000–587). In the *laments* (e.g., Ps. 44) the congregation cried to God for help in time of need; in their psalms of *thanksgiving* (e.g., Ps. 66) they thanked him for his aid; in their *hymns* (e.g., Ps. 96) they praised God as Creator and Lord of the world. In short, the Psalms were used in the temple cult.

But, secondly, a number of psalms belong within the context of the New Year Festival. The events which feature in these psalms, the distress which sparks off a lament or the help for which thanks are given to God, were events in the cultic drama of the New Year Festival. Thus when we read in a number of psalms (e.g. 47; 93; 95–100) of Yahweh's enthronement, there is reference to a performance which was actually enacted in the temple. The enthronement of Yahweh was not primarily either an event of the primeval era which the worshippers tried to recapture, or something that was expected at the end of days. Yahweh's enthronement was primarily an event that was experienced 'now' in the cultic drama of the New Year Festival.

A cultic drama[2] is composed of two elements, the sacral actions and the sacral words; the participant undertakes a number of pre-scribed sacral actions, or 'rites', such as dance, mime and so forth. The rites are accompanied by a series of prescribed sacral words which interpret the rites, and which the rites in turn symbolize. It is to these sacral words, which constituted a part of the cultic drama, that we shall apply the term 'myth'. Myth is 'the spoken part of ritual'.[3] This definition of myth as an element in cultic drama must not be construed too narrowly. A review of the critical discussion of the Ras Shamra texts indicates that the word 'drama' has been understood somewhat too literally (see above, pp.16 ff). The Ba'al myth is thought of as a play consisting of a series of scenes and acts, and scholars sometimes imagine that the texts were really performed, that specific individuals actually appeared in the temple and acted out the roles of the various gods, or in other words, that they actually uttered the words and performed the actions which are recorded in the texts.[4] Scholars have frequently held, for example, that it was the king who played the role of Ba'al as the dying and rising god of fertility.[5]

There is admittedly much to be said for this view of the texts from Ugarit. Experience, however, has shown that the distance between myth and rite can, to an external observer, be greater than the theory just indicated would suggest. We do know that *Enuma Elish*, the Babylonian epic of creation, was a mythical component of the *Akitu* festival (see above, pp.13 ff); but in the late form of the ritual as we have it today, the myth is first employed on the fourth day of the New Year Festival, when the *urigallu*-priest recites *Enuma Elish* to Marduk.[6] The distance between myth and rite is even greater in the Roman Catholic Mass, in which, by the use of quite simple means, the priest symbolizes the sacrifice of Christ on Golgotha. In the baptismal ceremony too the priest sprinkles water three times on the head of the child, an action which is paralleled by the mythical language of Rom. 6.4:

> We were buried therefore with him by baptism into death, so that as Christ was raised from the dead by the glory of the father, we too might walk in the newness of life.

What actually occurs in cultic drama is that the reality of myth is made immediate. When myth is employed by the cult, whether it is enacted as a 'real' drama or merely recited, the participants in the cult re-experience the events of the myth. The salvific actions of God are repeated in the cultic drama; creation and salvation are actualized for the cult participants. It is for this reason that the texts of Israelite worship often employ the word 'today'. One such 'today' is probably to be found in Ps. 118.24, which should be translated:[7]

> It is today that Yahweh acts;
> we shall rejoice and be glad *now*.

The stock example of this 'today' is the Greek Orthodox Easter greeting, 'Christ is risen!', to which the reply is 'Yes, he is risen indeed today:' When on Christmas morning we sing:

> O come, all ye faithful,
> Joyful and triumphant,
> O come ye, O come ye to Bethlehem,
> Come and behold him,
> Born the King of angels,

if we mean anything by it all, it is that we experience in this service our own journey to the city of David, and ourselves participate in the adoration of the new-born Saviour. Thus we conclude:

> Yea, Lord, we *greet* thee,
> Born *this* happy morning;
> Jesu, to thee be glory given;
> Word of the Father,
> *Now* in flesh appearing. . .

'*Adeste, fideles*' thus illustrates the cultic application of myth by its employment in a psalm. The English worshippers stand quite peacefully in their places while they sing of their journey to Bethlehem.

Myth may be activated cultically in at least three ways: (i) It can be 'acted out' through a series of rites, which step by step symbolize the events of the mythical plot, as in the Ba'al myth from Ugarit. (ii) It can be read aloud, and one may conceive how the various rites may be interpreted by a myth either before or after the reading itself, as in the case of *Enuma Elish* during the *Akitu* festival. (iii) Or it may be actualized when the congregation sing a psalm.

All in all, the psalm takes its natural place in relation to a cultic drama; in this God's saving actions are symbolized by the rites, which thus emphasize the fact that the drama is *God's* activity. However, man has occasion to speak, either before or after the divine action: in the psalms of lament the congregation cry out to God for aid and comfort, just as in the songs of thanksgiving they thank him for his assistance. In the hymns they praise God as the one who both can and will extend help. Thus the psalms represent the congregational response to God's actions.

Moreover, the psalms often contain reference to individual details of myth. Larger or smaller fragments of myth are, for example, present in a number of hymns as a foundation for the songs of praise ('O sing to Yahweh a new song, for he has done marvellous things!', Ps. 98.1). This characteristic is of special importance when we have to do with the Jerusalem New Year Festival during the period of the monarchy. Here we have only a very limited amount of source material at our disposal. We only have the Psalms; moreover, there is no explicit indication of ritual, as in the case of the Babylonian festival.[8] Nor, for that matter, are we presented with one coherent myth as in Babylon and Ugarit (see above, pp.13 ff.). We have only a number of hymnic fragments embedded in various psalms, and thus our supposition that these fragments allude to a cultic drama is purely hypothetical.

Isolated passages in the Psalms point directly to a cultic drama with the words, 'Come and see!' Thus in Ps. 46.8:

> Come and see the works of Yahweh,
> how he spreads terror in the earth.

Subsequent verses inform us what sort of works are alluded to above:

> He makes wars cease to the ends of the earth;

> he splinters the bow, shatters the spear,
> he burns the shields with fire (Ps. 46.9).

It is a reasonable supposition[9] that the liturgical use of this psalm entailed some sacral actions (rites) which symbolized the sacred words describing the works of Yahweh in v.10; it is these rites the congregation are invited to come and see. The phrase 'Come and see the acts of God' has a similar usage in Ps. 66.5.

Yet another indication of the cultic drama is to be found in Ps. 48. The psalm itself informs us that it was composed for cultic use, since vv. 12f. refer to the sacred procession in which the worshippers are enjoined to march around Zion, to count its towers, observe its ramparts and pass through its citadels. Before they are summoned to march in the procession they confess:

> As we heard (it), so have we seen (it)
> in the city of our God, of Yahweh the Lord of Hosts,
> which God establishes for ever (v.8).

The subject of the verse is something people have both heard and seen; it is accordingly very tempting to apply the 'heard' to the traditional cult myth,[10] and the 'seen' to the rites by which the myth was actualized. The concluding phrase of the verse suggests that the content of the myth was God's protection of his city Jerusalem. This interpretation of v. 8 can be reinforced by reference to v. 9, which we translate as follows:

> God, we have made us a likeness of your act of grace
> in the midst of your temple.

If it is correct to translate the Hebrew word (*dimmīnū*) in the sense 'to make a picture, likeness', which is its root meaning,[11] then this passage refers directly to the cultic drama in which the content of the myth, Yahweh's act of grace, must have been acted out or mimed.

As we have already observed, the Jerusalem New Year Festival has not survived in its entirety; we have only an assortment of fragments of myths preserved in those psalms of thanksgiving and hymns which we have chosen to regard as expressing the community's response to the divine action which takes place in the myth. Fragments of myth, some larger, some smaller, are cited in these responses as the motivation for the songs of praise. In what follows, we shall attempt to bring together some of these fragments of myth as a pattern.[12]

The creation myth

The nucleus of the Jerusalem Festival is the concept of Yahweh as Lord and Creator of the world. We encounter this understanding of Yahweh's role in such unqualified expressions as Ps. 96.5 ('All the gods of the peoples are idols, but Yahweh has made the heavens') and Ps. 95.3a,4–5):

> For Yahweh is a great God. . .
> In his hand are the depths of the earth,
> the peaks of the mountains belong to him.
> The sea is his. He has created it.
> His hands have formed the dry land.

A somewhat more 'mythological' image is depicted in Ps. 24.1–2:

> The earth is Yahweh's and its fullness,
> the world and its inhabitants;
> for he has founded it upon the sea,
> and established it upon the ocean currents.

In this passage we meet the old Israelite notion of the world as a great disc which Yahweh has placed in the midst of the ocean, as in Ps. 104.5–7. In other psalms we find the sea (*yām*) or the ocean current (*nāhār*; also river) personified as the opponent of Yahweh. Creation takes the form of a battle against the sea. This creation battle myth is detectable, albeit in somewhat reduced dimensions, in Ps. 93.3–4, in which the threats of the ocean current (RSV 'floods'; Heb. *nāhār*) are in vain, because Yahweh is mightier than the breakers of the sea (*yām*). There is no doubt that this passage really does refer to such a battle, since this is clearly to be seen in two laments in which confidence in Yahweh is expressed by direct citations of the creation myth. In Ps. 74.12–14:

> God is my king from of old,
> who works salvation in the midst of the land,
> You frightened away the sea (*yām*) in your power,
> crushed the heads of the dragons on the waters.
> You crushed the heads of Leviathan,
> gave them as food to the beasts of the desert.

In Ps. 89.9–12 we read:

> You do rule despite the sea's (*yām*) arrogance.
> You forced its foaming waves to be still.
> You crushed Rahab like a skewered thing,
> you sunder your enemies with your powerful arm.

Heaven belongs to you, yours is the earth,
you founded the earth and its fullness.
You created north and south,
Tabor and Hermon rejoice in your name.

We should recall that Leviathan and Rahab are the Hebrew names for the chaos monster ('the dragon'), whom Yahweh destroys in the battle at the creation. In other passages, such as Ps. 104.6, the chaos power bears the name *t^ehōm* (RSV 'the deep/cosmic deep'), which is a direct loan from Accadian Tiamat, the monster we encounter in the Babylonian epic of creation (see above, p.14). The Babylonian texts leave no doubt that the waters of the ocean in its destructive aspect are personified as the chaos power.

Thus in the drama of the New Year Festival the Israelites experienced the events whereby Yahweh slew Leviathan *anew* and repeated the creation event, when he made his 'work of salvation in the midst of the land' (perhaps in the temple?), Ps. 74.12. The repetition of the myth of creation surely also expresses the view that the Creator God sustains the created world against all of the threatening powers which are ranged against it.[13]

It would be pointless to attempt to decide what sorts of rites may have been employed to actualize the myth; however, we do happen to know that the cultic furniture in the temple included something called *yam*, a 'Sea' (I Kings 7.23–26).

As we suggested above, the Israelite myth of creation was a special case of the general oriental creation myth, which in Babylonia was expressed in the myth of Marduk's battle against Tiamat (see above, p.14). We encounter the same myth in the Canaanite sphere in the Ugaritic text which describes Ba'al's battle with and victory over the chaos power, which is called both Yam ('the sea') and Nahar ('the current' or 'flood'). It may be doubted whether the Ugaritic text actually implies the thought of a creation in the primeval era.[14] However, it must at all events be conceded that the victory of Ba'al over Yam represents 'creation' in the sense of sustaining the created world against the threats of the chaos powers.

We do not know whether the Israelites in the desert before their entry into Canaan possessed an understanding of Yahweh as Creator God. If they did, then after the entry into the land this concept came to be expressed in terms of a mythology which they must have straightforwardly borrowed from the Canaanite population. It would be reasonable to suppose that this appropriation of Canaanite mythology took place in Jerusalem, where El Elyon ('the Most High

God') was already worshipped in pre-Israelite times as the Creator of heaven and earth (cf. Gen. 14.18–20).[15]

It has often been asserted that the concept of God's creating the world by means of his word was a uniquely Israelite characteristic. It is certainly true that we meet this idea in the late version of the creation myth in Gen 1. God's creative word is also present in Ps. 33.6–9:

> By the word of Yahweh the heavens came into being,
> by the breath of his mouth all of its host.
> As in a waterbag he gathered the waters of the sea,
> placed the deeps in storehouses.
> All the world fears Yahweh,
> the inhabitants of the world tremble because of him;
> for when he speaks, it happens,
> when he commands, it stands there.

To this we should add that the creative word was originally an element in the battle myth; it is the threatening or exorcizing word which introduces the battle.[16]

This creative word is preserved in a more 'primitive' form in Ps. 104.5–9:

> He has founded the earth upon its columns,
> so that it will never topple.
> The deep covered it like a cloak,
> the waters stood above the mountains.
> It fled from your threat,
> was frightened off by the thunder of your voice,
> raced up mountains and down into valleys
> to the place you had determined for it.
> You made a boundary it cannot cross over,
> so that it will not again cover the earth.

We ought perhaps parenthetically to remark that for the author of Ps. 33 the creative word of Yahweh is the word by which he also maintains righteousness and justice (vv. 4–5).

The exodus myth

The world which God has created is the right one; it is the world in which the people speak the right language (Hebrew), and in which their customs and *mores* are in agreement with God's will. It is the world in which the king is the chosen of God (cf. Ps. 89.20ff.), even his own son (cf. Pss. 2.7; 89.27f.), who sits on the throne at the right hand of God (cf. Ps. 110.1). In Hebrew the same word is used to signify both 'world' and 'country'; in this connection we should recall that the temple in which the Psalms were employed was a national shrine, and that the Psalms were an expression of the official state religion. Thus Ps. 33 continues, 'Happy are the people whose God is Yahweh' (v. 12; cf. 89.15).

To the people of Israel their history was naturally integrated with myth. The creation was really complete only when Yahweh had led his people into their land. Thus the passage over the Sea of Reeds (the 'Red Sea'), the decisive salvation event of the people's prehistory, is represented in mythic categories, as a variant of the creation myth, in which 'Rahab' is used as a code name for Egypt, as in Ps. 87.4 and Isa.30.7. Moreover, the hymn which the 'historian' has the people sing after their dangerous crossing (Ex. 15.1–18) was originally a psalm from the New Year Festival.[17]

The exodus myth is present in the book of Psalms in a number of passages, among them Ps. 66.5a,6:

> Come and see the acts of God. . .
> He has turned the sea into dry land;
> they went across the river on foot,
> let us then rejoice in him. . .

The creation and exodus myths are so closely related that it can at times be difficult to determine which one is meant. Both of them speak of the divine protection of organized Israelite society against all encroaching powers. Thus a gradual transition from one theme to the other is possible, just as the creation myth cited above (Ps. 74.12–14) continues in v. 15, 'You did dry up the ever-running rivers.'[18] However, we do have an unambiguous example of the exodus myth in Ps. 114.1–4:

> When Israel went out from Egypt,
> Jacob's family from the stammering[19] people,
> then Judah became his (God's) sanctuary,
> Israel his kingdom.
> The sea saw it and fled,
> Jordan drew itself back,
> the mountains leaped like rams,
> the hills like lambs.

The interpretation of myth in historical categories has often been held to be a specifically Israelite characteristic. Against this it should be said that an understanding of history which sees it as the chosen field of action of God (or the gods), or one which understands historical events as manifestations of divine intervention, was by no means limited to Israel alone.[20] However, we should probably regard it as distinctive that the historical occupies so prominent a position in Israel's cult mythology; in any case, the fact that it is these particular historical events that are the centre of attention is indeed specifically Israelite.

In the actual exodus myth it is a single event drawn from the prehistory of the people, the passage of the Sea of Reeds, which is depicted in mythic categories. At times the field of view is broadened so as to include psalms in which the effusions of praise span the whole range of Yahweh's saving acts throughout history. We have examples of such encomiums in Pss. 105, 106, and 136; these recount the path of salvation history from the creation to the entry into of Canaan. Ps. 78 even brings the historical retrospect up to the time of the election of David.

We should not imagine that the pageant of salvation history was enacted step by step as a cultic drama;[21] however, it is clear that the confession of Yahweh as the God of history had an established place in the liturgy, as Ps. 44.1 indicates:

> God, with our own ears we have heard,
> our fathers have told us (about it):
> you performed a deed in their time,
> in the days of old (cf. Ps. 22.4–5).

Similar confessional accounts of the mighty acts of God are of course numerous outside of the Psalms, in such texts as Deut. 26.5–9; 6.21–24; Josh. 24.2–13; Neh. 9.6–31. Deut. 26 retells the saving history from the patriarchal Jacob narrative ('a wandering Aramean') to the entry into Canaan. The cultic use of this passage emerges clearly from its context; it was surely a confession intended to be used in conjunction with the offering of the first fruits.

It would be tempting for us, who live in a culture in which the written word plays a significant part, to regard such texts as Ps. 78 and Deut. 26.5–9 as secondary summaries of the traditions of the Pentateuch. The reality, however, is probably the opposite, namely, that the saving history originally belonged to the cultic confession of Yahweh as the God of history, and that it was only after centuries of development that its content was shaped into the great literary composition of the Pentateuch. This literary composition was constructed upon a basis consisting of the very few central motifs (the exodus from Egypt, the sojourn in the desert, and the entry into the land) which are listed in the cultic confession in Deut. 26.5–9.[22]

The myth of the battle with the nations

The Psalms were composed for use in the worship of the Jerusalem temple; indicative of this is the fact that they are distinguished by expressions of an almost ecstatic love:[23] 'One thing I shall ask of Yahweh, that I seek: that I may dwell in Yahweh's house all my life' (Ps. 27.4). These feelings for Yahweh are transferred in the sort of transitional movement characteristic of 'primitive' religion, to the temple as the place where he reveals himself, and to the city in which the temple stands. Both temple and city are thus ultimately subsumed under the name of Zion, as we read in Ps. 48.1–2:

> Great is Yahweh, and he is highly praised,
> in the city of our God on his holy mountain.
> Beautiful in height (?), a joy to all the earth,
> the mount of Zion in the farthest north,[24]
> the city of the great king.

Another declaration of love to Jerusalem stems from a later time (Ps. 137.5–6):

> If I forget you, Jerusalem,
> let my right hand forget (?).
> My tongue will cleave to my palate
> if I do not remember you,
> if I do not set Jerusalem above my highest joy!

The city of Jerusalem plays a central role in the variant of the cult myth which has been called the *myth of the battle with the nations*.[25] This myth is held to describe in story form Yahweh's providential care for Zion. In it all the kings of the earth amass their forces in an attack on Jerusalem and are on the verge of taking the city, when – just as the crisis is about to culminate – Yahweh reveals himself and saves the city from its enemies; Zion may thereafter be assured of security. An example of this story is found in Ps. 48.4–7; v. 4 presents the attack of the nations:

> See the kings assemble,
> they journey forth together.

Then Yahweh reveals himself; vv. 5–7 describe the effects of this theophany on Jerusalem's enemies:

> As soon as they see it, they are struck with fear,
> they flee in panic.
> Terror seizes them there,
> pangs as of a woman giving birth.

With the east wind you crush
the ships of Tarshish.

Again the verses describe events which the congregation have
both heard and seen; they are accordingly able to confess in v. 8,

As we have heard (it), so have we seen (it),
in the city of our God, Yahweh the Lord of Hosts;
God establishes it for ever.[26]

The close kinship of the myth of creation to that of the battle with
the nations is apparent in Ps. 46, in which the threat which impends
upon Israel is first described in cosmic dimensions (vv. 2–3) and
subsequently takes on political contours (vv. 5–6).
Ps. 46.1a, 2–3:

God is our refuge and strength. . .
Therefore we do not fear when the earth heaves,
and the mountains fall into the depths of the sea,
when its waters foam and seethe,
and the mountains tremble with its power.

vv. 5–7 continue:

God is in the city, it will not fall,[27]
God will help her at the turn of morning.
The nations rage, the kingdoms collapse.
He lets his voice sound
so that the earth trembles.
Yahweh of Hosts is with us,
our bulwark is the God of Jacob.

In earlier psalm research it used to be customary to attempt a
'*zeitgeschichtlich*' interpretation, i.e. one in terms of contemporary
history, of such psalms as 46 and 48;[28] the events of which they
speak were assumed to be external, political phenomena. Thus these
psalms would be held to describe an actual attack on Jerusalem
which was frustrated only in the nick of time. It would be appropriate in this instance to refer to the situation in 701, when the
Assyrian King Sennacherib attempted in vain to conquer Jerusalem;[29] Pss. 46 and 48 may very well have originally been used in
such a context.

It is possible to explain the fact that both the catastrophes and
the saving acts of Pss. 46 and 48 are depicted in mythic categories
in the following manner: in Ps. 46 the congregation express their
confidence that the God of the creation myth will also aid them in

their political extremity; in Ps. 48 they give thanks for the political salvation they have experienced, which they perceive as a confirmation of the language of the cult myth about the God who is both Creator and Saviour. Thus the motif of the battle with the nations expresses the experience of the community that the conceptual world of the myth is in fact reality.[30] This characteristic has been described as a 'historicizing of myth', but one could with equal justice term it a sort of 'mythologizing of reality', by which the community understand an external, historical emergency by means of the categories of myth and so receive confidence in divine assistance. This mythologizing of reality is without doubt a factor one must take into account in the interpretation of the Psalms.[31]

But in spite of the conceivable validity of the above interpretation, we feel that a 'purely cultic' analysis would be more appropriate to Pss. 46 and 48. In other words, we suggest that the events recounted in these psalms are primarily events which were experienced by the community in the cultic drama. For one thing, it is in these two very psalms, 46.8 and 48.8 (see above, pp. 65f.), that we meet the clearest references to the cultic drama. Moreover, it is evident from the way the myth of the battle with the nations speaks of death and salvation that the events alluded to in these psalms are too vast to refer to mere external, political events. Comparison with Ps. 2, in which the nations' attack is depicted as the rebellion of unfaithful vassals against the 'great king' in Jerusalem, is instructive. The psalm is introduced by the bemused and ironic query of the great king in vv. 1–3:

> Why are the nations unquiet,
> and the peoples make plans doomed to failure?
> The kings of the earth set forth,
> the princes assemble in council
> against Yahweh and against his anointed:
> Let us burst their chains
> and cast their ropes from us!

This image, in which the kings of the earth are conceived as rebellious vassals of the great king in Jerusalem, never possessed any shadow of actuality in the course of Israel's history, and was valid only in the world of myth. It expresses the idea that the king in Jerusalem, as son of the Creator God (v.7), has at least in terms of the ideals of Israelite theology a claim to make on the overlordship of the world (vv. 8f.). Thus the myth of the battle with the nations implies an ideology which may at least to some extent be expressed in the words '*Dei gratia fidei defensor, omnium Britanniarum rex*'.[32]

To what has been said above we should add that a purely cultic interpretation of the myth of the battle with the nations is not solely a product of Scandinavian psalm research; strenuous efforts along the same lines have also characterized recent English and German studies.[33] We should also like to advise against an overly sharp distinction between the methods of the contemporary history approach and purely cultic investigation, since according to both methods it is the external, political reality about which the cult myth is thought to speak. Thus, when the myth of the battle with the nations was actualized with the help of the cultic drama in the New Year Festival, it was a means of expressing confidence in the willingness of the Creator God to intervene even in situations of external, political crisis. Such psalms as 46 and 48 would by this means have achieved renewed significance if, for example, they were employed in the New Year Festival of 701. In spite of the arguments which maintain that the Psalms are an expression of traditional cultic language, and hence very difficult to date, we should like to emphasize the fact that each psalm must have come into being at a particular point in Israel's political and religious history. It is unthinkable that an author in the process of reformulating the myth of the battle with the nations for the New Year Festival could have avoided being influenced by the actual political situation of his country. In this sense at least, a 'historical' interpretation must be considered justifiable.

Ultimately, however, we feel that the form of the myth as we have it today in Pss. 46 and 48 antedates 701, since it is already presupposed by the oldest stratum of Isaiah.

Isaiah's proclamation from the 730s, as it is preserved in Isa. 7–8, can be construed as an actualization of the ideology of the myth of the battle of the nations (see below, pp. 116ff.). If this understanding of Isa. 7–8 is correct, then the myth of the battle of the nations is at least some decades older than 701; in all probability it is several centuries older.

The exodus myth is a specifically Israelite form of the myth of creation found all over the ancient Near East (see above, pp. 69ff.). The myth of the battle with the nations is a Jerusalem version of the same myth. In reality, there is nothing at all which suggests that this reshaping of the myth took place in historical Israelite times. We should rather regard the myth of the battle with the nations as a portion of the mythological legacy which Israel acquired from the Canaanites by making Jerusalem, the former sanctuary of El Elyon ('God the Most High' of Gen. 14.18–20), the centre of her worship.[34] The fact that the myth is everywhere concerned with the city suggests that it came into being at a time when Jerusalem was a city state, as was the case before David's conquest. In this connection it is significant that the old divine epithet Elyon ('the Most High') is preserved in Ps. 46.4, and, finally, the assumption that Israel appropriated the myth from the Canaanites in Jerusalem makes it possible to explain certain similarities between the myth and a number of characteristics of ancient Near Eastern cult mythology.

There are, of course, no exact parallels to the Jerusalem myth of the battle with the nations; however, as early as the Sumerian literature we have examples of hymns which praise the god for his victory over political enemies; moreover, these praises depict the divine victory in metaphors which belong to the creation myth. According to a hymn to *Martu*:[35]

> He has [ordered up] the 'seven' winds,
> lets it [rain] fire,
> he annihilates (the enemy) in strife and battle,
> [he flashes] like lightning,
> constricting terror of him seizes the evil-doer,
> [he overwhelms him] [like] a stormwind.
> The city he curses does not [get] its power back.
> On behalf of the King he annihilates all
> foreign lands which do not give way.
> To the good shepherd,[36] whom he chooses in his heart,
> Martu, An's son, brings his help.[37]

Mythical motifs which are 'lacking' in the Psalms

Up to this point we have spoken quite unconcernedly of a hypothetical New Year Festival in Jerusalem; moreover, we have done so without answering the objection that the OT nowhere specifically names a New Year Festival.[38] Our reply is that the festival in question is in fact well attested by the sources; it is the great autumnal festival which the OT calls either the harvest festival, or the Feast of Booths, as in Ex. 23.16; 34.22; Lev. 23.33–36; Deut. 16.13–16; Num. 29. In I Kings 8.65 it is simply referred to as 'the Feast'. Moreover, when we specifically use the term New Year Festival of this event, it is not without evidential support in the texts, since Ex. 23.16 mentions the feast at 'the beginning of the year', while Ex. 34.22 refers to the feast of ingathering at 'the turn of the year' (NEB).

However, the term 'New Year Festival' is primarily a technical term; it signifies that the Jerusalem Feast of Booths was similar in kind to those New Year festivals with which we are otherwise familiar from the literature of the Near East. It followed the cultic ritual pattern which we know from the New Year celebrations of Babylon and Ugarit.[39]

The cultic ritual pattern of the Canaanite New Year Festival is known to us from the texts from Ugarit. Three major motifs, besides the battle with the dragon, which we dealt with above (p.68), are present in this pattern:

1. the death and resurrection of the fertility god, Ba'al;
2. his sacred marriage with the goddess Anath;
3. his enthronement as king over gods and men (see above, pp.16).

Two of these motifs – the concept of the death and resurrection of the god and that of his marriage – are absent from the OT Psalms as we have them today.[40]

There are three possible explanations of this absence from the Psalms of two themes which were so central to Canaanite mythology. One is the nature of the original Yahwistic faith; Israel seems never to have forgotten that her God was actually from Sinai. There were characteristics of the desert god which rendered it impossible for him to be completely assimilated to the figure of the Canaanite fertility god. For example, Yahweh was *lord* of fertility, which meant that unlike Ba'al he could never be fully identified with fertility, which dies in the summer drought and is restored by the autumn rains. Yahweh was also the 'living' God (whatever this expression may have signified in a Canaanite context), which in the OT meant 'the God who never dies'. Moreover, he was characterized as a *jealous* god, who therefore would tolerate no divine consort by his side.[41] In this connection we should note that even if in some of the Israelite rural shrines Yahweh more closely approximated to the figure of Ba'al, at least in Jerusalem the cult of Yahweh succeeded in preserving something of the exclusiveness of original Yahwism. Admittedly, the OT itself bears witness to the fact that Israel worshipped Ba'al, Ashera, the sun, moon, stars, and 'the whole host of heaven' in the temple during the period of the monarchy (II Kings 21.3–5; 23.5–12); none the less, it remains true that the Yahweh we meet in the Psalms is neither a dying nor a rising god, nor does he have a divine consort by his side, because he has retained some of his characteristics as originally a desert god. It is clearly a reasonable supposition that the royal reforms of the cult of which we read from time to time (I Kings 15.11–15; II Kings 18.3–6; 22–23) had their origin in circles that were connected with the temple.

A second explanation is that we only know the Psalms in a censored form. The unity which in spite of all differences characterizes these OT texts is the result of redaction by the Yahwistic priesthood.[42] This suggestion is reinforced by the account in II Kings 23.4–14 of Josiah's purification of the Canaanite elements from the Jerusalem cult; it would be unthinkable that these Canaanite elements should not at the same time have been removed from the texts used in the cult.

The third and most interesting conjecture assumes that the motifs of the death of the god and of his marraige were 'missing' from the Jerusalem cult even before the Israelite period. The syncretism we encounter in the Psalms is seen as having occurred by fusion with the Jebusite cult of El Elyon. If El Elyon was not a dying and rising god, and if his cult did not include a sacred marriage, it would not occasion surprise if the same were to hold true of the cult of Yahweh in Zion.

We already know from Gen. 14.18–20 that El Elyon was worshipped in Jerusalem in the pre-Israelite period; however, we have no reason to suppose that Ba'al, the Canaanite fertility god, was worshipped in Jerusalem until a relatively late date [43] (cf. II Kings 21.3; 23.5; cf. also II Kings 8.18,27). One could ultimately explain the eventual absolute supremacy of Yahwism by the assumption that the special character of its Israelite element, i.e., the notion that Yahweh is a jealous God, had been preserved in the process of fusion. Of course, one could also explain it as a late formation in the Canaanite element of this syncretism.

There is no doubt that each of the explanations offered above contains each in its own way, something of the truth of the matter. In any event, it is certain that neither the concept of Yahweh as a dying and rising god, nor the idea of a divine consort by his side, has any place in a reconstruction of the mythology of the Jerusalem New Year Festival based on the Psalms as we have them today.

The enthronement of Yahweh

If two of the motifs which, as we suggested above, played important roles in the Canaanite New Year Festival are not demonstrable in the Psalms, then at least the third theme, the enthronement of the god, is amply attested by these materials. The Psalms contain a series of richly varied descriptions of Yahweh's arriving at the temple and mounting his throne as the King of gods and men. The enthronement of Yahweh is indeed so central to the New Year Festival that Scandinavian studies often refer to this event as the Enthronement Festival of Yahweh.[44]

One such depiction of Yahweh's arrival as God and King, or his theophany, is evidenced by Ps. 97.1–5:

> Yahweh is king, let the earth rejoice,
> let the many coastlands be glad.
> Clouds and darkness are round about him,
> righteousness is the foundation of his throne.
> Fire goes forth before him
> and consumes his enemies round about him.
> His lightnings illuminate the world,
> the earth sees it and trembles.
> The mountains melt like wax before Yahweh,
> before the lord of all the earth.

A similar theophany is contained in Ps. 18.6–15, a psalm of thanksgiving in which the worshipper offers his thanks for divine assistance:

> In my distress I called out to Yahweh,
> cried for help to my God.
> He heard my voice in his temple,
> my cry found its way to his ears.
> Then the earth shook and trembled,
> the ramparts of the mountains heaved and shook,
> for he was angry.
> Smoke went up from his nostrils,
> devouring fire from his mouth,
> and coals flashed from him.
> He lowered the heavens and came down
> with darkness beneath his feet.
> He rode upon the cherub and flew,
> hovered on the wings of the wind.
> He made darkness for his concealment,
> for his dwelling (? RSV: 'canopy') around him,
> dark bodies of water, saturated clouds.
> From his radiance hastened his clouds before him,
> hail and glowing coals.
> Yahweh thundered from the heavens,
> Elyon ('the Most High') let his voice resound

with hail and glowing coals.
With his arrows he clove them,
with flashes of lightning he frightened them.
The bottom of the sea was seen,
the foundations of the world stripped bare
by your threat, Yahweh,
by the blast of the breath of your nostrils.

A number of traditional elements are to be found in this theophany.
Fire and smoke are the normal accompaniments of Yahweh's revelations, as in Ps. 97.2f.; Isa. 6.4; I Kings 8.10. In Ps. 18.13 Yahweh
is pictured as a god of thunder; it is ordinarily assumed that this
and similar metaphors (cf. Pss. 29; 68.33) stem directly from the
Canaanite Ba'al traditions, in which the god reveals himself in the
thunderstorms of the autumnal rainy season.[45]

We can accordingly compare Ps. 18.13 with the following Ugaritic
text, in which Ba'al is represented as the god of thunder in practically the same words:

He opens the cleft of the clouds
and Ba'al lets his holy voice be heard.[46]

Matters are, however, more complicated than they might at first
appear to be, since the context in which Yahweh is depicted as God
of thunder also preserves the divine appellation Elyon. This leads
us to believe that in pre-Israelite times the thunder motif was
attached to the figure of the 'Most High God', El Elyon, and that
it was only secondarily transferred to Yahweh.[47] Finally, the theophany itself contains allusions to the creation myth as it appears in
the form of the battle with the dragon; by his threat alone, Yahweh
frightens the sea away, so that the foundations of the earth can be
seen. Nothing less would do when the worshipper, as in Ps. 18, has
cried to the Creator God for help.

We saw above (pp.69ff.) how the realm of the historical provides
Israel's cultic mythology with important features. This fact is again
evident in a number of theophanies which represent Yahweh's
descent from Sinai. An example is Ps. 68.7–8:

When you proceed, O God, before your people,
when you advance through the desert,
the earth shakes, and the heavens drip, before God,
it is Sinai,[48] before God, the God of Israel

(cf. Deut. 33.2; Judg. 5.4–5). The Canaanite idea that the god is

the bringer of fertility is to be seen in, among other passages, the
theophany in Ps. 65.9–13:

> You look after the land, water it,
> make it extremely rich.
> The stream of God is full of water,
> you provide their grain,
> yes, even thus you provide it.
> You water its furrows, smooth out its ridges,
> you soften it with rain, bless its seed.
> You crown the year with your fullness,
> the trail of your chariot oozes fatness.
> The waste pastures flow,
> and the heights clothe themselves with joy.
> The meadows clothe themselves with sheep,
> the heights wrap themselves in grain.
> In joy they burst out and sing.

Against the hypothesis of an Enthronement Festival of Yahweh
as a permanent part of the New Year Festival, it has been objected
that it is difficult to imagine how a cult which rejected the use of
images should have been able symbolically to depict the enthronement of the god.[49] Our reply is that the nature of all cultic procedure
is such that quite magnificent mythical events are capable of representation by very simple means in the rites.[50] Indeed, even if the
only thing that 'actually' went on in the temple was the singing of
such psalms as 97.1–5; 18.7–15; and 65.9–13, it would have been
possible for the congregation in song to experience the theophany
of Yahweh as a cultic reality.

Moreover, we do in fact know that the Jerusalem temple contained at least one requisite of the cult, the function of which was
precisely to symbolize the presence of God: Yahweh's sacred chest,
the Ark of the Covenant.[51] According to the traditions of the Pentateuch the Ark originated during the Israelite nomadic period,
when it led the tribes in their wanderings (cf. Num. 10.33–36). In
this connection we read that whenever the Ark 'set out' Moses said,
'Arise, Yahweh, let your enemies be scattered and your opponents
flee from you!' and when it halted he said, 'Return, Yahweh, to the
ten thousand thousands of Israel!' Similarly, we read in I Sam. 4
that during the war with the Philistines the Israelites brought the
Ark to their encampment, which drove the Philistines to panic,
since 'God has come into the camp' (vv. 6–8). Of course, the Ark
was subsequently captured by the Philistines, but only because
Yahweh permitted it, and chs. 5–6 describe the triumphal progress

of the Ark through Philistia until the Philistines were compelled to return it to the Israelites, who established it on a temporary basis at Kiriath-Jearim. There it remained until David brought it to Jerusalem (II Sam. 6). The central act of Solomon's consecration of the temple consisted of his ordering the Ark to be brought from the city of David to the holy of holies in the temple (I Kings 8.1–11).

Thus the most natural understanding of Pss. 132, 47, and 24 is that during the New Year Festival the Ark was carried in procession into the temple, thus symbolically re-enacting the arrival of Yahweh at his sanctuary.[52] Ps. 132 belongs at the beginning of the procession; according to this psalm, the only cultic act consisted of a repetition of David's procession before the Ark into Zion (II Sam. 6); here the role of David would have been played by the reigning monarch. The psalm is introduced by a prayer for the king (vv. 1–5); thereafter, the messengers arrive who have been out searching for the Ark (v. 6): 'Lo, we heard of it in Ephrathah, we found it in the field of Ja'ar.'[53] Then the decision is taken to convey the Ark to the temple (v.7) and to urge Yahweh to bestir himself: 'Rise up, Yahweh, to your resting place (go), you with your mighty Ark!' (Cf. Num. 10.35; Ps. 68.1.) Verse 9 mentions that the priests are correctly robed, and that the worshippers are rejoicing. Finally the psalm modulates into an intercessory prayer on behalf of the royal line (vv. 10–18).

Ps. 47.5–7 paints a vivid picture of what was experienced during the procession:

> God goes up amid rejoicing
> Yahweh (goes up) to the sound of the ram's horn.
> Sing for God, sing,
> Sing for our King, sing!
> God has become King of all the earth,
> sing a maskil![54]

Psalm 24 describes the arrival of the procession at the temple gate. The psalm is introduced by a hymn to Yahweh as Creator (vv. 1f.; see above, p. 67). Then the congregation enquire who may be allowed to enter the temple. The doorkeepers reply, only he who has clean hands and a pure heart. The congregation reply that they do possess these qualities (vv. 3–6; cf. Ps. 15). They twice demand that the gates be opened (vv. 7 and 9):

> Lift up your heads, you gates,
> raise yourselves, you ancient doors,
> that the King of honour may go in.

The doorkeepers twice inquire who it is that seeks admittance and when, after the second question, the congregation names Yahweh of Hosts, the gates are opened (vv. 8 and 10). Having entered, the participants must have placed the Ark in the inner room of the temple (the 'holy of holies') or, in mythological language, Yahweh was seen to remount his throne, as in Ps. 47.8:

> God has become King[55] over the nations,
> God has seated himself upon his holy throne.

Accordingly, the entire world is invited to participate in doing homage to the new king on Zion (cf. Pss. 96.6–12 and 98.4–8); the nations, the entire natural world, and even the divine world are urged to pay him homage.

The king in the mythology of the Psalms

There was a temple in Jerusalem; it was constructed in the tenth century at the instance of King Solomon. According to the popular opinion of the time, it was the king himself who had built the temple;[56] moreover, this project was only a part of the comprehensive building programme whose purpose was to serve the honour of the king and thus enable him to exercise his power. It is apparent from the account in I Kings 6.37 – 7.8 that the temple was only a detail in a much more ambitious programme, but it was nevertheless a significant detail. The political function of the temple cult was to keep the kingdom orientated towards the Davidic royal house.[57] The words which Amaziah used of the temple at Bethel, 'this is the king's sanctuary, and a temple of the kingdom' (Amos 7.13), might very well have been used of the Jerusalem temple; the temple and the royal power belonged together.

There was a temple in Jerusalem; psalms were sung there; also, it was a state sanctuary, just as the psalms expressed the official religion of the state. This close connection between king and temple is expressed by, among other passages, Ps. 132.11–14:

> Yahweh has sworn to David
> an oath he will not break:
> Of your heirs I will put
> kings upon your throne.
> If your sons adhere to my covenant
> and my commandments, which I shall teach them,
> their sons shall also sit for ever on your throne!
> For Yahweh has chosen Zion,

desired it for himself for a dwelling:
Here I will live; I have desired it.

Ps. 132 is one of the psalms we employed above (p.82) in aid of our reconstruction of the ritual of the New Year Festival. The total context of the psalm indicates that it was usual in the festival to remind Yahweh of his covenant with David.

One such psalm, in which Yahweh is explicitly reminded of the full extent of his promises to David, is Ps. 89.19–37. In other words, yet another element in the ritual of the New Year Festival was the renewal of the covenant between the deity and the royal house. A similar renewal of the covenant by which Yahweh had bound himself to a specific king on the event of his coronation undoubtedly underlies Ps. 21.2–7:

Yahweh, the king rejoices in your strength,
greatly he exults in your salvation.
You give him what his heart desires,
what his lips crave you do not refuse.
You come to meet him with auspicious blessings,
(you) place a crown of gold upon his head.
He asked life of you; you gave it to him,
a long row of days without end.
His honour is great through your salvation,
you endow him with greatness and majesty.
You make him a constant blessing,
you give him a share in the joy
one has at being near you.
For the king trusts in Yahweh,
because of the faithfulness of the Most High
he does not falter.

Whether this psalm was used year after year on the occasion of a renewal of the covenant, or whether it was composed with a particular occasion[58] in mind, it is an excellent example of the experience of the royal coronation. Theologically, it is Yahweh himself who imbues the king with power, just as it is Yahweh himself who places the crown on his head (v. 3), who makes him a 'constant blessing' for the people (vv. 3,6), and who promises him 'eternal' life (vv. 2,4; cf. Pss. 72.5; 89.29,36). The coronation rite is a distinctive sign that the king finds his strength in God (cf. vv. 1,7).

In the Psalms the reigning king acts as a divine figure.[59] The king is Yahweh's anointed; he is designated 'son of God' (Pss. 2.7; 89.27f.); moreover, in an isolated passage he is straightforwardly addressed as God ('Your throne, O God, endures for ever', Ps.

45.6).[60] As son of the Creator God, the king has a claim to make on the overlordship of the world (Ps. 72.8; cf. Ps. 89.25). In 'reality' he is the great king and the other kings are merely his vassals; if the latter rebel,[61] the king can point to the warrant of his authority in the assurances of the Creator God, as in Ps. 2.7–9:

> I will tell of what Yahweh has determined.
> He said to me, 'You are my son,
> I have given birth to you today.
> You have only to ask and I will give you
> the nations as your property,
> all of the earth as your possession.
> You shall crush them with a staff of iron,
> shiver them in fragments like potsherds.'

The king's power comes from God; he rules in agreement with the divine will. The fundamental principle of his government consists in the Godgiven rules for the structuring of society – what the OT calls 'righteousness'. Thus Ps. 45.6f.:

> A staff of righteousness is your royal sceptre.
> You love righteousness and hate injustice.
> Therefore God, your God, has anointed you
> with the oil of gladness above your fellows.

The justice of the sovereign is emphasized to an exceptional degree in his care of those who are poorly situated in society. A Ugaritic text depicts the mode of government of a Canaanite king with the words, 'He judges the cause of the widow and tries the case of the orphan.'[62] In like manner, Ps. 72.4, 12–13 says of the Jerusalemite king:

> He secures the cause of the wretched among the people,
> rescues the poor,
> but crushes the man of violence.
> He delivers the poor man when he cries for help,
> and the wretch who has no helper.
> He has pity on the weak and the poor,
> He saves the lives of the needy.

To this we should add that the king's reign is characterized by overwhelming fertility. When the king is everything he is ideally supposed to be (which, incidentally, he invariably is in the cultic texts of the royal temple), the rain falls at the right time and the grain grows tall. Ps. 72.6–7,16 says of the king,

> He comes like rain falling on withered meadows,

like rainstorms that water the earth.
In his days the righteous flourishes,
and there will be great fertility[63]
as long as the moon endures.
There is abundance of grain in the land,
up to the tops of the mountains.
Its fruit waves like Lebanon,
and they sprout forth (?) from the city
like the herbs of the earth.

Thus the Psalms indicate that in Israel the ancient Near Eastern royal ideology was to a large extent assimilated for domestic use and applied to the Davidic king. The king was regarded as God's representative on earth. In the New Year Festival the covenant between the deity and the royal line, that is, the covenant which was constitutive of society's political and social life, was renewed.

For this reason a cultic prophet originally pronounced assurances to the king in the ritual of the New Year Festival (Ps. 110.1–2):

Yahweh says to my lord:
'Sit at my right hand,
until I have made your enemies
like a stool for your feet!'
Yahweh reaches out with your mighty sceptre from Zion.
Reign among your enemies!

In recent OT research there is fairly general agreement that the Psalms bear witness to Israel's appropriation of the widespread Near Eastern royal ideology. In Scandinavian Psalm research there is also general agreement that the royal ideology found expression in the ritual of the New Year Festival: at some point in the course of the liturgy a cultic prophet must have come forth and announced that Yahweh had elevated the king, in words resembling those which are preserved in Ps. 110.1–2 (above).

On the other hand, there is at present no consensus on the vexing question of whether or not the ritual originally contained a section in which the king was for a time subject to a cultic humiliation. More precisely, did the New Year Festival enjoy a dramatic character in the sense that the royal ritual was originally composed of two elements: (1) the divine rejection of the king, and (2) Yahweh's re-acceptance of him as the rightful ruler of his people. We know that oriental New Year festivals often contained this dramatic aspect; the festival was a play about life and death in which, through experience the festival, one experienced that life is renewed through

death. Thus Ba'al, the Canaanite fertility god, dies only in order to
revive (see above, pp.16ff.). The myth of the battle with the nations
at the Jerusalem New Year Festival (see above, p.72) tells how they
attempt to storm Jerusalem, only to be prevented at the last
moment. Did the royal ritual of the Israelites possess a corresponding two-member structure?

Further, did the Israelite royal ritual at one time include the
element which scholars have referred to as the 'cultic suffering of
the king'?[64]

The cultic suffering of the king

We have an example of the cultic suffering of the sacral king preserved in the parts of the ritual of the Babylonian New Year Festival
which have survived down to our times. In the ritual of the fifth
day the king takes part in a scene which, according to C. J. Gadd[65]
should be reconstructed as follows:

> The king now entered for the first time. Escorted in by priests
> he was immediately left alone before the statue. Soon the high-
> priest[66] appeared and took away from him his regalia, his
> sceptre, ring, and crooked weapon, and his crown, which he
> placed upon a stool before Marduk. Next he struck the king a
> blow on the cheek, pulled his ears, and forced him to kneel
> before the god. In this humiliation the king had to recite a sort
> of 'negative confession':
>
> > I have not sinned, O Lord of the lands, I have not been
> > unregardful of thy godhead,
> > I have not destroyed Babylon, I have not commanded her
> > ruin,
> > I have not shaken E-sagila, her rites have I not forgotten,
> > I have not smitten the cheek of the people in my charge
> > . . . nor caused their humiliation.
> > I take thought for Babylon, I have not beaten down her
> > walls.
>
> To this the chief-priest replied with a message of comfort and
> blessing from the god; he would hear his prayer, increase his
> majesty, and strike down his enemies. Hearing these words, the
> king might now reassume his sovereign bearing, and at once
> received back from the god, by the priest's hands, his insignia
> of royalty. Once more, however, the priest was to strike him
> upon the cheek and that not softly, for a sign was to follow –
> if tears came into his eyes, Bel was gracious, if not Bel was
> wroth; the enemy would arise and work his ruin.

We should like to maintain that a number of OT Psalms[67] can best be understood if we assume that their original *Sitz im Leben* was a corresponding phase in the Israelite royal ritual, in which Yahweh for a time rejects his king. The best example of this is offered by Ps. 89.38–45,[68] which bemoans the fact that Yahweh has rejected the king:

> You have cast off and rejected,
> have dealt in anger with your anointed one.
> You have revoked the covenant with your servant,
> have despised his crown (by casting it) to the earth.
> You have breached all his walls,
> have laid his fortresses in ruins.
> All passers-by do plunder him,
> he is (the object of) the derision of his neighbours.
> You have raised the right hand of his enemy
> have gladdened all his opponents.
> You have allowed his sharp sword to fail,
> nor have you sustained him in battle.
> You have allowed his (royal) brilliance to fade,
> have cast his throne to the earth.
> You have cut short the days of his youth,
> and clothed him with disgrace.

Ps. 89.38–45 thus constitutes a lament for the king's tragic situation in the cultic drama of the New Year Festival. Verses 46–51 are a prayer for Yahweh to intervene in this, the king's direct extremity and save him; it is clear that in the ritual Yahweh has granted the petition of the king. Afterwards, we should assume, the congregation sang psalms of thanksgiving in which Yahweh was praised for his salvation. Ps. 18 gives an example of such thanksgiving;[69] vv. 4–6 recall the king's extremity:

> The cords of death were wound about me,
> the streams of annihilation terrified me,
> the cords of the realm of death entangled me,
> the snares of death met me.
> In my distress I called out to Yahweh,
> cried for help to my god.
> He heard my voice in his temple,
> my cry made its way to his ears.

It is characteristic of the psalm that the king's distress is here given cosmic proportions; thus the sufferer had descended to the realm of death before his cry could make its way to Yahweh's heavenly temple.

The description of salvation (vv. 7–15) has therefore similar cosmic perspectives (see above, p.80) which demonstrate that it was the Creator God whom the sufferer had called upon for help. The account of the king's rescue continues in vv. 16–19:

> He reached out from on high and took me,
> drew me up out of the numerous waters.
> He preserved me from my powerful opponent,
> from my enemies; they were too strong for me.
> They met me in the day of my distress,
> but Yahweh became my stanchion:
> he led me out into the open country,
> he tore me free, because he takes pleasure in me.

It is probable that Pss. 22, 69 and 88 are also related to the tradition of the king's cultic suffering. Here again, it is significant that the calamity depicted has mythical overtones. In Ps. 22. 12–21 the sufferer is surrounded by wild animals; in Ps. 69.1–2 he is ringed in by the waters of Sheol, and in Ps. 88.6 he cries out to God from the deeps of the Pit. It is equally significant that it is in reality Yahweh who is responsible for the king's plight, though this is sometimes modified by the implication that the king's suffering is undergone for Yahweh's sake, as in 69.7,9. In Ps. 89.51 it is clear that it is Yahweh's enemies who are (albeit momentarily) triumphant; however, most often the cause is ascribed to Yahweh's having turned against the king (Ps. 88.6–8); thus the sufferer laments that Yahweh has abandoned him as in Ps. 22.1. Yahweh is furthermore said to have rejected his anointed one in Pss. 88.14 and 89.39ff.; cf. 44.9,23.

There are two possible objections to the understanding of Pss. 89 and 18 here adumbrated. First, one could hold that it is a long way from Babylon to Jerusalem, and that it is thus improper to use the Babylonian New Year Festival, which we incidentally only possess in a very late form, to reconstruct individual segments of the Jerusalem ritual. To this point we reply that we are *not* able to reconstruct the Jerusalem ritual; the Babylonian parallels we have cited are only intended to show that it is *possible* for the theme of the king's cultic suffering to have been expressed in the rites of the New Year Festival.

Similarly, we affirm that it is a valid procedure to attempt to understand Pss. 89 and 18 as originally having figured in a cultic drama. Whether the Babylonian rites were used in the Jerusalem New Year Festival or whether some radically different rites were employed, we shall never know; nor shall we ever be able to determine if the Israelites were satisfied merely to sing Ps. 89, followed by Ps. 18.[70]

The second objection to our thesis notes that there is a considerable discrepancy between the cosmic descriptions of these psalms and the actual disaster and salvation of the Babylonian rite, in which the king's cultic suffering is expressed by a blow on the cheek. Again, we should insist that the nature of cult is such that the great events of myth are capable of expression by essentially very limited means.[71] Moreover, it would be incorrect to assert that the decisive rite of the Babylonian ritual consisted of a blow on the cheek of the king. Rather, it consisted in the stripping of the king of his regalia by the *urigallu*-priest, who then placed them in the chapel before Marduk (he got them all back later). The possible significance of a rite of this kind to a 'primitive' society, which placed a high value on external trappings, is not difficult to imagine. Moreover, a parallel procedure is explicitly detailed in Ps. 89.38–45.[72]

Some scholars have attempted to carry out a 'historical' analysis of Pss. 89 and 18,[73] according to which the events the psalms describe are conceived of as external, political events. Thus the enemies of which these psalms complain are thought to have been actual, historical opponents. In this vein, Ps. 89 has been seen as stemming from a day of repentance and prayer that was held after a military defeat; conversely, Ps. 18 has been seen as an element in a festival of thanksgiving following a victory. The fact that the crisis and deliverance which figure in Ps. 18 are both expressed in mythical categories could accordingly be regarded as a variant of the 'mythologizing of reality' to which we alluded above (p.74). The community must have understood the external, historical emergency in mythical categories and seen their salvation as confirmation of the language of the cult myth which depicts God as Creator and Deliverer.

It is not possible to distinguish sharply between the 'historical' and the 'pure cultic' interpretations presented above, since even the 'pure cultic' view sees these psalms as relating to external, political reality. If the king's cultic suffering was 'enacted' during the New Year Festival, it served as an expression of the confidence of the congregation that the God of the royal line would also succour *them* in their hour of need. Moreover, if a day of repentance and prayer was observed at a time of acute political crisis (and we are informed by Jer. 36.9 that this did sometimes occur), then its purpose was by lament and prayer to depict the political emergency in religious language; that is to say, in mythical categories. There is in reality no very great difference between these two interpretations.[74]

However, we should like to point out that there is nothing whatever in Ps. 89 to suggest that it was written for a service of prayer and repentance after a military defeat.[75]

The special view of the king which is expressed by these psalms is a peculiarly Israelite variant of the ancient Near Eastern royal ideology. Accordingly, if there are any passages at all in the OT which might lead one to suppose that Israel had appropriated the mythological cult language of the Canaanite cult of El Elyon, these are they.[76] The idea seems indeed to be directly announced in Ps. 110.4, which speaks of the renewal of the king's sacerdotal status:

> Yahweh swears, he does not regret it:
> 'You are a priest for ever
> in the same way as Melchizedek.'

According to Gen. 14.18, Melchizedek was the name of a Canaanite king of Jerusalem, a contemporary of Abraham. He is supposed to have been king of 'Salem' (= Jerusalem), and priest of El Elyon. Thus in Ps. 110 it is the lordship and priestly status of this Jebusite king which the Davidides claim to have inherited.

Conclusion

There is one particular interpretation of the cultic drama of the New Year Festival which ceaselessly haunts the periphery of our study: the understanding of the cult as magic. Especially for us who live in a world without myth it is tempting to regard the cult myth as a magic word that creates what it names, and the rite as a magical action that functions according to an inner dynamic. When the reappearance of Yahweh at his sanctuary or the suffering and restoration of the sacral king are depicted in the cultic drama of the New Year Festival, it is easy for us to feel that the Israelites must have attempted to force God to realize their own hopes and expectations by means of sacral actions and words.[77]

The myths and rites of the New Year Festival could also be described as an expression of the congregation's profound sense of their dependence on the Lord of life. When in the cultic drama the king experienced cultic suffering, that is, when he was first cast off and subsequently restored as Yahweh's rightful king, who ruled over Yahweh's peculiar people, the entire ritual might be construed as signifying that the king of Israel owed all his power to Yahweh.[78]

It is really a question of the authenticity of the cultic experience. If the congregation truly experienced the rejection of the king as a reality which during the course of the ritual at least hypothetically offered the possibility that Yahweh might, for once, choose not to hear the king's prayers, then we may say that they encountered Yahweh in the New Year Festival as a personal god who was both other and more than a mere expression of personal hopes and expectations.[79]

We may therefore be inclined to reject any suggestion of magic in connection with this living religion.[80]

It is true of religious as well as ordinary language[81] that neither contains clear expressions by means of which we can objectively determine the authenticity of an experience. In this case, we have left to us for consideration only the religious language of the Israelite New Year Festival, and the only procedure open to us is to analyse this language. We can see that it differs in some particulars from the religious language that was employed at other sanctuaries in the Near East. We can also see that Israelite religious language employs to the full the conceptual world of myth, which the Israelites seem to have appropriated from their neighbours. It is possible that there were some myths or mythic motifs the Israelites were not capable of assimilating (see above, pp.76ff.), but they did take up myths as such and exploited their possibilities fully in those psalms which tradition has preserved for us.

However, when we arrive at the ultimate question as to whether this language is empty and formal, or whether it is an expression of genuine religious experience, we lack unassailable arguments, if the following should prove unacceptable: if a man (or group of men) recounts a religious experience he claims to have had, then as long as he says nothing which directly militates against our doing so, the most obvious thing to do is to take him at his word.

Jerusalem was conquered in 587 by Babylonian soldiers; the king and the greater part of the upper classes were led into exile in Babylon. The priestly leaders were executed and their followers accompanied the nobility into exile. The treasures which had been stored in the temple were confiscated and the building itself, along with all the other buildings in the city, was set on fire.[82] But people continued to sing psalms.

In the little book called Lamentations, which tradition has appended to the book of Jeremiah, we find the clearest possible example of what we have termed the 'mythologizing of reality' (see above, p.74). According to Lamentations it was not the Babylonians

who destroyed Jerusalem; it was Yahweh himself who had rejected
his sanctuary (Lam. 2.1):

> He has cast down from heaven to earth
> Israel's splendour
> and forgets his footstool
> in his day of wrath.

Lam. 3.55 depicts the catastrophe in words that might have been
borrowed from the ritual of the cultic suffering of the king:

> I call out your name, Yahweh,
> from the depths of the Pit.

In this situation, in which Israel had been deprived of her political
independence and her cultic institutions, and in which the individual was forced to eat his bread in peril of his life (Lam. 5.9), the
people, or rather the pitiful remnant of them, had no more to cling
to than the wistful pronouncement, 'perhaps there is hope' (Lam.
3.29). Lam. 3.21–24:

> This I take to my heart,
> therefore I shall hope:
> the faithfulness of Yahweh is not ended,[83]
> his mercy is not past.
> It is new every morning,
> great is your faithfulness.
> 'My portion is Yahweh', says my soul,
> therefore I will hope in him.

4

MYTH IN THE PROPHETIC LITERATURE

Knud Jeppesen

The relationship of the prophets to cult and myth

Tradition has regarded the prophets as spokesmen whose preaching has demonstrated its enduring value. The prophetic books, which constitute about a quarter of the OT, are primarily collections of prophetic texts which are ascribed to a variety of authors. To this collection we should add a number of stories in the historical works of the OT which concern either named or anonymous prophets. Common to all of these texts is the fact that under certain defined situations the prophet delivers an oral announcement, an oracle.[1]

The prophetic proclamation is principally the promulgation of a *religious* message; the prophet is ordained of God and is accordingly qualified to announce 'Thus says Yahweh'. The task of the prophet is to convey to his contemporaries that which God intends they should understand as his will.

Yahweh is often represented as the God of history who revealed himself to the Israelites in the events of the past:

It was I who destroyed the Amorites before them
whose height was like the height of cedars,
and who was as strong as the oaks;
yes, I destroyed their fruit above
and their roots beneath.
It was I who led you up from the land of Egypt
and let you wander forty years in the desert
so that you shall inherit the land of the Amorites (Amos 2.9f.)[2]

The prophets represent the God who chose the Hebrew people before they made their entrance into a cultural sphere in which the fertility cult was dominant; in their proclamation they depict this encounter with Canaanite culture and religion and its attendant consequences as a most serious betrayal of the relationship with Yahweh which had arisen as a result of the election in the desert or, according to another tradition, in Egypt:

> Like grapes in the wilderness I found Israel,
> like early fruit on fig trees, as a first fruit
> I saw your fathers.
> They came to Ba'al Pe'or,
> and consecrated themselves to *outrage*,
> so that scarecrow gods became their lover (Hos. 9.10).[3]

Nor is Israelite apostasy confined to an isolated occasion; the prophets understand only too well that Canaanite influence is a continuing problem. Jeremiah, who lived over five hundred years after the people's flirtation at Ba'al Pe'or, has them confess in a lament of repentance (3.21ff.) that they have sinned generation after generation, 'from our youth even to this day . . . we have not obeyed the voice of Yahweh our God' (v. 25). Their sin has consisted in participation in the Canaanite or Canaanite-influenced cult on the high places. Moreover, the people admit, and their admission surely reflects the prophet's own point of view, that this cult has not yielded all that one might have expected in the way of fertility in stall, field, and bed:

> The *outrage* devoured the produce of our fathers
> from our youth:
> their flocks and herds,
> their sons and daughters (Jer. 3.24).

While the prophets are thus seen as in principle defenders of the truly Israelite, we must recognize that much of what they stand for derives from the Canaanite milieu. In the first place, we must suppose that, as it appears in the OT, prophecy is one of the institutions which the Israelites took over under Canaanite influence.[4] Moreover, analysis of prophetic language demonstrates that the prophets tend to make use of the available religious language of the day, that is, the language of worship as reflected in the Psalms. But as we observed in the previous chapter, the OT cultic texts are interpenetrated by myths and mythical conceptions of Canaanite and hence of Near Eastern provenance. We should therefore expect the Hebrew prophets, as defenders of truly Israelite values, to advocate the rejection of myth (see p. 4 above). In reality, however, we find that they take neither whole nor half measures to dissociate themselves from the mythological conceptions of the Psalms. They appear never to consider whether one or another mythological notion is genuinely Israelite or not; rather, it seems to be more important to them that the theology and world-view of a particular myth should correspond to their own position. Should these features so correspond, the prophets seem to be otherwise unconcerned as to the origin of the myth.

Thus myth and mythical conceptions are ubiquitous in the prophetic literature. However, where the Psalms tend to employ myth thematically and universally, the prophets tend to use it to illumine topical and often critical situations.

There exists no opposition in principle between the cultus and the prophets;[5] on the contrary, we are forced to assume that at least some of the prophets emerged from temple circles. It would also be incorrect to imagine that this connection with the temple nullified their freedom;[6] rather, the prophets seem to have been free, among other things, to allow the understanding of life conveyed by a particular myth to appear in a new and original context. Without giving thought to the origin of the myth, a number of prophets attempt to startle their audience into a new awareness by using the myth in a novel way and thus lending it new impact. On this point, at least, there seems to have been scope for considerable independence.

The function of a cult is invariably, in one way or another, to establish harmonious relations between the divinity and the community, or, to employ a heavily loaded word, to procure *salvation*. However, harmony and salvation are not obtained without risk; before the full achievement of salvation is it necessary to actualize the sequence of dramatic events of which the myth speaks: the battle against the powers of chaos must be experienced (see pp. 11f., 63f.).

The Israelite cult provides for the possibility of the people's being judged and condemned by Yahweh. In Ps. 95, one of the Enthronement Psalms, the people are the object of a divine admonition, conceivably mediated by a cultic prophet: 'O that *today* you would hearken to his voice!' (Ps. 95.7b).[7] Later verses refer to earlier generations who were disobedient to Yahweh. There is special mention of those Israelites who were not convinced by Yahweh's saving acts in the desert, and who therefore incurred the judgment: 'They shall not enter my resting-place' (v.11b).

The same possibility applies to the people, the cultic community: they may also be excluded from the resting-place, which in the cultic context signifies the temple in Jerusalem. However, to be excluded from worship is equivalent in mythic language to being separated from God. Psalms of penitence and lament reveal that this separation implies loss of vitality, righteousness and salvation (cf. Ps. 6); again in cultic terms this means that one may not participate in the rite which expresses fellowship with God, that is, the pilgrimage, the procession to the temple.[8]

The point is apparent in Ps. 42, in which the speaker remembers sadly how he 'went with the throng and accompanied them in procession to the house of God'[9] (v. 4a). The actual situation of the psalmist is placed in opposition to this: he 'thirsts for God, for the living God' (v. 2).

It seems, however, that a tendency to superficiality is inherent in the nature of the cult; the dramatic element fades away and forgiveness is pronounced more or less automatically, as long as the demands of ritual are scrupulously observed. Here again we encounter the prophetic freedom to emphasize the gravity of the judgment, which is to say that there is always the possibility of a prophetic 'No!' if the conditions of salvation are not present. Or we could say, in language associated with the history of religions, that the tendency to break down the distinction between 'historical time' and 'sacral time' (see pp. 8f. above) is more prominent in the prophets than in the everyday expressions of the cult. The 'today' of cultic language cannot be contained within the four walls of the temple; on the other hand the historical 'today' must not be envisioned in isolation from the cultic situation.

If in secular life the members of the cultic congregation are sinners, the holy day, the day of Yahweh, will mean not salvation but judgment:

> Woe to you who have great expectations of the day of Yahweh!
> Why do you desire the day of Yahweh?
> It is darkness and not light! (Amos 5.18),

'I know', says Amos, 'how many are your transgressions and how great are your sins' (5.12); the people are guilty of sins of corruption, social injustice and so on. But there is still a ray of hope:

> Hate evil, love the good,
> see that law is observed in the gate!
> Perhaps Yahweh, the God of Hosts,
> will be gracious to the remnant of Joseph (5.15).

However, Amos regards it as highly probable that the judgment against them has already been determined and pronounced. We find the same background to Jeremiah's invective against the Jerusalem temple and its cultus (cf. Jer. 7 and 26); Yahweh's commandments are not being kept (7.9), and Jeremiah's contemporaries are not a whit better than the generation of desert-wanderers they are so eager in the cult to condemn (7.22ff.).[10] Thus there is no longer either power or significance in the congregational refrain, as Jeremiah knew it, which was probably a feature of the temple service:

> This is Yahweh's temple,
> Yahweh's temple,
> Yahweh's temple (7.4).

According to Jeremiah, in the historical context in which these words are uttered they are based on a deception; they are 'lying talk' (7.4).

In what follows we shall attempt to examine a number of mythological motifs in a more systematic way. We shall not attempt to account definitively for these phenomena, because of the large amount of material and our present limitations of space. However, a treatment of some distinctive motifs should indicate with sufficient clarity just how central myths are to the prophetic cast of thought.

It is impossible to evaluate the particular situation of each prophet separately in the course of our systematic analysis.[11] We can here only emphasize the special characteristic of the prophets: that their activities cannot be meaningfully sundered from their contemporary historical situation; without some correspondence between daily life and the ideals of the cult the latter are devoid of significance.

Psalms like 46 and 48, 89 and 18 become most intelligible when interpreted in terms of the cult, but as we have seen, we cannot wholly ignore the historical interpretation (see pp. 73ff., 90f., above). On the other hand it could be said that the prophets are to be understood historically, but that at the same time we cannot ignore the cult which was the background of their activities. It is therefore important to note that the two oldest of the writing prophets, Amos and Hosea, were active not in Jerusalem but in the Northern Kingdom.

The case of *Amos* is relatively uncomplicated, since the cult with which he is familiar does not differ greatly from the one into which we gain insight in the Psalms. This is probably because Amos was

Judaean by birth (cf. 1.1; 7.12), so that his cultic milieu was the temple in Jerusalem;[12] but it would also be intelligible if the cult in Bethel was in fact closely related to that of Jerusalem; both were in any case royal sanctuaries (see p. 83 above).

Hosea, on the other hand, reveals in his preaching that he is confronted by a form of Yahwism in which the fertility myths play a much greater part than they do in the Psalms; his background can thus hardly be the same as Amos's, i.e., Bethel. We have more probably to do with a cult in Samaria.[13]

All the other prophets operate against the background of the temple in Jerusalem. Admittedly, a few of them were active in isolation from it, since they prophesied during the Babylonian exile. This applies, for example, to the prophet responsible for the proclamation of Isa. 40–55, the so-called *Deutero-Isaiah*. It is considered one of the most certain results of critical scholarship that these chapters do not come from Isaiah ben Amoz, who prophesied under a series of Judaean kings in the eighth century BC. The Second 'Isaiah' is clearly spiritually related to the eighth-century Isaiah the son of Amoz, but the decisive difference between them lies in the fact that the Second Isaiah lacked the opportunity to relate to a living cult in Jerusalem, with its share of cultic use and abuse.

It is thus all the more important for our purposes that the preaching of Deutero-Isaiah is predicated upon the mythology of the New Year Festival (see pp. 76f. above), since this fact demonstrates the extent to which these mythological conceptions were rooted in Israelite theology.

Judgment and salvation

The prophets are representatives of Yahweh, the God whose nature is revealed in the cult and myths of Israel; however, they are at the same time members of the very nation to whom they are sent. They do not merely utilize the language and myths of the people without according recognition to the underlying perceptions of these myths. The thought of Israel as the chosen people of God is a primary Israelite presupposition; they are the people on whose behalf Yahweh has acted in history and whom he will continue to protect against the dangers of the world – as long as they themselves desire it. One of the principal reasons the prophets like to emphasize the seriousness of the myths of judgment is their fear that the people will, by their foolishness and recalcitrance, destroy their chances for this future.

The covenant, which both prophets and people consider to be the basis of relationship between Yahweh and Israel, is a two-sided covenant; therefore the people's sinful behaviour can have only the direst of consequences:

> I know you alone of all the races of the earth;
> therefore I will punish you for all your transgressions (Amos 3.2).

It is the prophetic duty to proclaim this message, for the people's sake. Here ends the prophetic freedom. It is bad enough in the first instance that the prophets must prophesy 'war, famine, and pestilence against many countries and great kingdoms' (Jer. 28.8);[14] but it is worse by far that they are sometimes forced to proclaim judgment upon their people, or elements of them. Thus Micah cries out, after his prophecy of the fall of Samaria:

> Therefore I will lament and moan,
> let me go naked and bare of foot,
> let me make lamentation like the jackals,
> sorrow like the ostriches (Micah 1.8).

Undoubtedly, the prophet has not always had an easy time of it. Sometimes the people to whom he is sent protest, 'Do not preach ... one should not preach of such things' (Micah 2.6); these are often individuals who, according to Yahweh, 'have rebelled against me' (Ezek. 2.3). It is nevertheless the prophet's duty to 'speak my words to them, whether they hear or refuse to hear' (Ezek. 2.7).

At times the prophet is even commissioned to preach a message whose consequences are by design destined to be the opposite of conversion and salvation:

> Make the heart of this people fat,
> make their ears heavy, make their eyes stick shut
> so that they shall not see with their eyes,
> or hear with their ears,
> and understand with their hearts,
> so that he again will heal them (Isa.6.10).[15]

Ultimately, the prophet performs his errand because it is Yahweh's will that he do so; he is confident that Yahweh knows what he is about. On the other hand, it is of no avail to attempt to shirk one's duty in this respect: if Yahweh has determined that a message should be pronounced, then nothing will stay him, as Jeremiah acknowledges:

> You took me by force, Yahweh, and I let myself be taken,
> you seized me and prevailed (Jer. 20.7).[16]

Just as in the cult the aspects of both judgment and of salvation are present, so also the prophetic proclamation is not limited solely to the preaching of judgment.[17] When the prophets feel that the stipulations of the covenant have been fulfilled, it appears natural for them to employ those myths which describe happiness and salvation in an idealized future. When the time of punishment has elapsed, and its lessons are learned, there will come times in which

> every man shall sit under his vine
> and under his fig tree,
> and none shall spread fear about;
> for the mouth of Yahweh of Hosts has spoken (Micah 4.4).[18]

Nor can that future be envisioned without the temple of Zion and its worship:

> In that day shall the branch of Yahweh be beautiful and glorious, and the fruit of the land shall be great and lovely for those who have survived in Israel. The remnant in Zion and the survivors in Jerusalem will be called holy – that is, every one who has been recorded for life in Jerusalem. When the Lord shall have washed away the filth of the daughters of Zion and rinsed the bloodguilt out of Jerusalem with the spirit of judgment and the spirit of purification, then will Yahweh create over the whole of Mount Zion and over its congregation a cloud by day, and smoke and flaming fire by night. . . There will be a hut for shade by day from the heat, and for shelter from the storm and rain (Isa. 4.2–6).[19]

Death and resurrection

Gottlieb asserts (p. 77 above) that two important motifs of Canaanite mythology are absent from the Psalms. Specifically, these are the notions of the death and resurrection of the fertility god, and his *hieros gamos*, or sacred marriage, with the fertility goddess. In what follows we shall attempt to find traces of these conceptions in the prophetic literature.

An investigation of this kind would benefit from taking its point of departure in the preaching of Hosea; however, his writings offer no evidence of an attempt to place the concept of the death of Yahweh in the mouth even of his adversaries. This could conceivably indicate that even in the most 'Canaanite' of milieux, Yahweh remained untouched by the fertility cycle and its concomitants of death and resurrection. Alternatively, Hosea could well have found the whole notion so despicable that he refused to soil his fingers with it. However, the omission could equally well be merely coincidental,[20] since Hosea is not otherwise notably delicate in his references to Yahweh; moreover, it *is* possible in his works to discern some expressions suggestive of a North Israelite line of thought which is at least related to the myth of the death and resurrection of the god.

Hosea 10.5ff. has reference to the cult of the calf in Bethel; yet Hosea does not name Bethel, the 'House of God', but Beth–'aven, the 'House of the Evil power'. Hosea prophesies concerning the calves that they shall be destroyed by the Assyrians, and that this will naturally bring sorrow to the Israelites. This sorrow is not, however, depicted in neutral terms: the expressions employed are those which in Canaanite religion are associated with lament for the death of Ba'al and his descent to the realm of the dead.[21]

If we momentarily entertain the idea that the Israelites performed a rite corresponding to a myth of Yahweh's descent to the kingdom of death, this could plausibly have included the calf-figure, as symbol of the god, being crushed and obliterated.[22] If this was the case, Hosea's proclamation could be taken to signify: 'You have worshipped Yahweh blasphemously by – among other things – rites of sorrow and lamentation; but now Yahweh will visit a real sorrow upon you. The expressions you have used in your worship shall now come to mean something, for now you shall really have something to lament.'

It is also possible that a notion of the absence of (the dead) Yahweh is concealed behind the announcement that Israel will come with all her flocks to *seek* after Yahweh, but will not *find* him (Hos. 5.6). This passage could be taken to mean that the prophet says that what is 'mimed' (see p. 66 above) by the Israelites in the cult will, at some future time, become a tragic reality.

Finally, Hosea definitively rejects the use of the formula '*ḥay Yahweh*', 'as the Lord lives' (4.15). In the OT this expression figures as an oath (I Kings 1.29; 2.24, etc.), not least in the book of Jeremiah (4.2; 5.2, etc.), which, as we shall see in the case of the wedding metaphor, has other points of contact with the preaching of Hosea. In this case the phrase is used in the prophet's argumentation for the return of the people from their impending capitivity (Jer. 16.14f.; 23.7f.). Correspondingly, the prophet puts the expression 'as I live' in the mouth of Yahweh (Jer. 22.24; cf. Ezek. 14.16,18,20; Isa. 49.18). It is interesting to note that one of the passages in which Jeremiah uses the phrase *ḥay Yahweh* gives us a hint as to Hosea's reasons for forbidding its use. The context describes what will become of the 'evil neighbours' of Israel (Jer. 12.14ff.):

> If they will truly learn my people's customs.
> so that they will swear by my name, 'as Yahweh lives',
> *just as they taught my people to swear by Ba'al,*
> then shall they be built up among my people (Jer. 12.16).

From this we can conclude that Jeremiah was familiar with the oath *ḥay Ba'al*, 'as Ba'al lives', which the Israelites had presumably borrowed from their Canaanite milieu. Thanks to the modern text discoveries at Ras Shamra-Ugarit we now know that this oath in all likelihood did exist; one of the texts of the Ba'al cycle has El (the supreme god of the Ugaritic pantheon) say, 'Then I know that Aliyn Ba'al has revived.'[23] El thus expresses his awareness that Ba'al will, after his death, live again, and his choice of words indicates that we should regard the existence of the oath in question as highly probable. It is therefore possible that when Hosea takes exception to the expression *ḥay Yahweh*, it is because he knows the corresponding Canaanite expression, with all that it entails of Ba'al-associations. Clearly, the prophet would not wish these characteristics to be transferred to Yahweh.

While it thus seems likely that there were circles in the Northern Kingdom who celebrated the death and resurrection of Yahweh, this was not the case in Jerusalem (see pp. 77f.); there it was possible to use the phrase *El ḥay*, 'the living God' (Ps 42.2 quoted on p. 97 above) without danger of misunderstandings arising. It was possible for King Hezekiah to emphasize, against the Assyrians, that Yahweh was a living God (*'elōhīm ḥay*, Isa. 37.17; cf. v. 4).

It was as a living God that Yahweh had always presented himself throughout history. One can automatically assume that Yahweh will never die:

> Yahweh is God – that is certain! –
> he is the living God and the king of eternity (Jer. 10.10).

The 'other gods' did not fashion heaven and earth (v. 11), but:

> He fashioned the earth by his power,

established the world by his wisdom (v. 12).

Against this background, it is understandable that Jeremiah can without hesitation ordain rites of repentence and lamentation (Jer. 6.26) which originated in Canaan, even if we also know from Ezekiel's prophecies that Jeremiah's contemporaries also held mourning feasts for the Babylonian fertility god, Tammuz (Ezek. 8.14). It was apparently impossible at this period in Jerusalem to confuse Yahweh with a fertility god of this sort. It would by the same token be unreasonable to suppose that Deutero-Isaiah conceives of Yahweh as a dying God when he cries,

> Awake, awake,
> clothe yourself in power, O arm of Yahweh (Isa. 51.9),

even if 'sleep' is often used as a synonym for the death of the fertility god.[24] It was possible for Yahweh to 'cut Rahab in pieces' and 'pierce the dragon' (51.9) without, as a preliminary, having to die; this is indicated by the use in the Psalms of the myths dealing with these themes.

Even if Hosea was forced to deal with the conflict between Yahweh and Ba'al to a far greater extent than the Jerusalem prophets, so that he was compelled to reject any language or cultic drama which might suggest that Yahweh was a dying and rising Ba'al, he none the less felt free to term the Israelites 'sons of the living God' (Hos. 1.10). It is significant that this occurs at an important point in Hosea's preaching, where he breaks with the symbolic names which were given to his children by the harlot (see below, p.109). These names constitute a curse upon the people which, the prophet announces, will be dispelled by the direct agency of God.

Furthermore, the language of the myth of the dying and rising god is not restricted to the above-mentioned cases; it also figures prominently in Hosea's own preaching. The function of the suffering, death, and resurrection which take place in the divine world is to ensure that the people will enjoy fertility and plenty, which can be most clearly discerned in those passages in which the king undergoes cultic suffering (see pp. 87ff. above and 113 below).

It does not look as if Hosea and his opposition knew a form of royal suffering, or at least, such a tradition has left no imprint on his preaching. Nevertheless, the prophet does in fact get across the point that (cultic) suffering exists for the sake of the people, which Hosea understands – as perhaps his audience does too – to mean that the people participate directly in such suffering by means of vicarious participation in the rites of death and resurrection.

It is also conceivable that some of the rites of the cult should be understood as expressing the death of the nation. Perhaps in Hosea's place of origin what corresponded to the battle with the nations was a myth of the death and resurrection of Israel. Whatever the case may have been, Hosea does insert the following passage into the mouth of the people, after they have spoken of the sufferings which Yahweh has inflicted upon them at the hands of historical enemies (Hos. 5.13ff.):

> In two days he will make us alive,
> on the third he will raise us up (Hos. 6.2).[25]

After these sufferings, Yahweh will restore life to the people. But Hosea, as the spokesman of Yahweh, rejects such complacency (vv, 4ff.); the people do not have the right attitude, their sacrifices take place for the wrong reasons (v. 6), there is breach of covenant and unfaithfulness (v. 7), and so on:

> In Israel's house
> I have seen horrible things (Hos. 6.10).

Furthermore, there can be no question of the people's being saved in any automatic way:

> He rends, let him now heal;
> he strikes, let him now bind up! (Hos. 6.1).

In fact, Hosea even accepts the possibility that the people may die, because of their rebellion against Yahweh. The realm of death is a dominion to which Yahweh can consign Israel, and from which he will not rescue her without effort, and certainly not automatically. If the people should happen to experience death, they will also have occasion to taste of it:

> Shall I ransom them from Sheol?
> Shall I liberate them from Death?
> (understand: No, I will not!)
> Where is your plague, O Death?
> Where is your torment, O Sheol? (Hos. 13.14)
> (understand: Do your worst, I shan't hinder you!)

The last line of the verse could be taken to mean, 'I shall not see compassion before my eyes.'

Death must not be regarded as a harmless element in a wrong-headed worship of Yahweh; it represents an actual power which

Yahweh is able to wield against his people. But when death has been experienced and understood by repentance and by the genuine amendment of evil ways – which is by no means intended in any trivial sense (Hos. 14.2f.) – then Yahweh will again allow his people to flourish:

> I will heal (the result of) their apostasy,
> I will love them freely!
> My anger has turned away from them!
> I will be like dew to Israel,
> he shall blossom like the lily
> and put down roots like the tree of Lebanon,
> his shoots shall spread (to every side),
> and he shall be like the olive tree for beauty,
> and his fragrance shall be like Lebanon.
> They shall again dwell beneath my (?) shadow;
> they shall cultivate grain,
> blossom like the vine
> whose reputation is like the wine of Lebanon (Hos. 14.4–7).[26]

In the book of Hosea the proclamation of the reality of death is directly succeeded by a speech on life with Yahweh, and the consequences this will have for prosperity and fertility. Only death, which Yahweh in his sovereignty dispenses, and life, which he freely bestows, represent the myth which fulfils the people's need for fertility and plenty.

In the rest of the prophetic literature the myth of the death and resurrection of the nation is not especially evident; however, it does seem to be present in a text which has been preserved in a relatively late stratum, Isa. 57.3ff. It is true that the people are here primarily depicted in phrases which belong in the context of the myth of the sacred marriage, but there is one phrase which is of interest to our investigation. It says of the people (the woman, the harlot), 'you descended to Sheol' (Isa. 57.9). In the following passage this behaviour is regarded as disloyal to Yahweh (v. 11), and clearly in this context it signifies apostasy and the worship of other gods (v. 13).

In contrast to this, Ezekiel is able to use the myth of death and resurrection in a much more positive way, and within the framework of Yahwism. In the famous ch. 37 the prophet relates how he is seized by the hand of Yahweh and led to a valley filled with a litter of bones. At the command of Yahweh Ezekiel prophesies to these dry bones and discovers that Yahweh has the power to clothe the naked skeletons with tendons, muscles, flesh, skin, and hair, so that they become living people again.

This vision constitutes Yahweh's reply to the people's despair:

> Our bones are dried up,
> Our hope has withered,
> (the thread of our life) has been severed (Ezek. 37.11).

The prophet is to proclaim on behalf of Yahweh:

> See, I will open your graves,
> and lead you up from your graves, O my people;
> and I will bring you back to the land of Israel (v. 12).

Ezekiel's announcement was of momentous significance, not only because it became a presupposition of the later Christian teaching on the resurrection of the body, but also because it had immediate effects in its own period. It gave expression to that change of heart which was necessary for the people, before they could achieve sufficient maturity for the return to Jerusalem with confidence in Yahweh's desire to save. This joyous message was the presupposition which enabled the Israelite-Jewish religion to survive its exile in Babylon – and many exiles ever since.

The sacred marriage

Another major fertility myth is the myth of the sacred marriage, or *hieros gamos*, between the god and goddess. This myth, too, was unknown to the Jerusalem cult, at least as far as we can determine on the basis of the Psalms. The Deuteronomistic history suggests that there was a cult of Astarte inaugurated by Solomon (I Kings 11.5), which perhaps functioned continuously throughout the period of the monarchy until it was abolished by Josiah some three hundred years later (II Kings 23.13); even if this was the case the goddess can hardly have been regarded as the consort of Yahweh.[27]

In the Northern Kingdom, on the other hand, it is more likely that there were circles who worshipped a female divinity paired with Yahweh. Among the texts from the island of Elephantine on the Nile is one which implies that the Jews who were settled there worshipped two divinities besides Yahweh, of which at least one, Anath–bethel, was female.[28] Anath is the name of Ba'al's consort in Canaanite religion, and Bethel is suggestive of an origin in the Northern Kingdom. However, while the thought of Yahweh's possessing a divine consort was probably not equally repugnant to all

Israelite circles, we do not find it directly expressed in the OT, not even placed in the mouths of Hosea's opponents.

However, *hieros gamos* signifies more than just the heavenly marriage of the male and female divinities; it also embraces the marriage of the divine king (see pp. 83ff. above and pp. 114f. below) and his queen, the purpose of which is to ensure the permanence of the dynasty, and thereby the nation. Ultimately, it includes every sexual rite which fell within the sphere of the fertility ritual.[29]

The fertility rite was both familiar to and popular with Hosea's audience: its popularity was not merely a function of the fact that its participants were allowed to be 'immoral'. The symbolism of the rite is easily intelligible, since it is not difficult to grasp the connection between a sexual act and the concept of fertility. It is a rite which brings the individual into intimate contact with the process of creation reflected by the cult.

Hosea opposes Israelite participation in this sort of rite, and he protests against the dedication of young women to bridal rites in the cult:

> They sacrifice on the tops of the mountains,
> and make smoke upon the heights,
> beneath the oak, poplar, and terebinth,
> because the shade is good.
> Therefore your daughters play the harlot,
> and your daughters-in-law[30] commit adultery (Hos. 4.13).

Similarly, Hosea rejects the orgiastic cult which flourishes by the wine vat and the threshing floor, the sacred places of the fertility religion:

> Rejoice not, O Israel,
> do not exult like the peoples!
> You are playing the harlot away from your God,
> you love a whore's pay on every threshing floor.
> (But) the threshing floor and the wine vat
> are not their neighbour,[31]
> the new wine will fail them (?) (Hos. 9.1f.).

The prophet maintains that these rites do not lead to the expected result: 'no birth, no pregnancy, no conception!' (9.11). The people have failed to live up to the demands which have been placed upon them; they have not understood what it entails to be the son whom Yahweh has called up from Egypt (11.1) to be a prince among the peoples (13.1). They have forgotten that all that they have comes from Yahweh, all their material possessions, be they grain, wine or oil, or even the materials from which their idols are made (Hos. 2.8).

Against this background, we should expect that Hosea would exercise caution in his use of language so as not, for example, to employ the language of the fertility religion when he speaks of Yahweh. However, as we observed before, Hosea is not so delicate in these matters. In a brilliantly creative way he utilizes a myth which is fundamentally at loggerheads with Yahwism so that it speaks significantly of Yahweh and Israel. He depicts the relationship between God and people as a sort of sacral marriage in which the bridegroom says to his bride:

> I will marry you for ever;
> I will marry you for[32] the sake of righteousness and justice,
> for steadfast love and mercy.
> I will marry you for truth (Hos. 2.19f.).

The marriage, however, was a disaster! The promise of marriage cited above presupposes that the sentence of judgment, which we have suggested is implicit in the myth of death and resurrection, has been carried out. Until such time, according to the customs of Hosea's society, the marriage would be regarded as a failure. The prophet demonstrates this not only in words, but in the great symbolic action of his life: his marriage with Gomer, the harlot.[33] This action represents the relationship between Yahweh and Israel as essentially perverted; in relation to Yahweh the people are like a wife unfaithful to her husband. The sacred marriage has lost its sanctity because one of the members has other relationships in which she seeks the life that properly pertains to marriage.

Admittedly, the marriage of Gomer and Hosea bears fruit, but the children are children of harlotry, and their names are a nullification of the essential values which the Israelite relationship to God should have confirmed. Thus the elder son bears the name Jezreel, because blood-guilt attaches to that name (1.4); the girl is 'Not pitied' (1.6), and the younger son is called 'Not my people' (1.9). The names of the children represent the judgment which has been passed upon the people; this is proclaimed in ch. 2, in which sentence is passed upon the mother. The sentence will be enforced until the people 'shall know the Lord' (2.20).

Knowledge of the Lord is a central theme in Hosea's theology; it is one of the expressions of faith in Yahweh which is absent from the society in which he lives (4.1; 6.6). 'To know God' does not, to Hosea, merely signify a kind of intellectual assent to a factual proposition; rather, it means to know what God intends and to act in accordance with this knowledge.

Yahweh has attempted in vain to forgive the people:

> When I would restore the fortunes of my people,
> when I would heal Israel,
> Ephraim's transgression is revealed,
> and the wickedness of Samaria;
> they bring fraud to consummation (Hos. 6.11–7.1).

The prophet accordingly feels that the time has come to take a more drastic course; it would be useless for the people to attempt to build on their uncertain foundations: they must start all over again.

Still relying on the marriage metaphor, Hosea says that the husband will lead his wife by force out into the desert, where things will at last be put right (2.14).[34] This sojourn in the desert corresponds to that death-like state Yahweh inflicts on his people in order to save their lives: 'The realm of death is . . . closely related with the desert-land. The two belong together as the opposite of man. . . '[35] The woman is isolated in the desert in order to bring her low (2.15),[36] so that the original and more natural relationship can then be resumed:

> In that day, says Yahweh,
> you will call me 'my husband',
> and no longer call me 'my Ba'al';
> then I will remove the names of the Ba'als from her mouth,
> and they shall not be named by name again (Hos. 2.16–17).

There is thus no power in the fertility rites sufficient to save the people from Yahweh's punishment; nor can they bestow life, over which Yahweh alone is Lord. Life is the consequence of Yahweh's free gift of love (14.4) and must be received as such before a lawful marriage can be carried out. What follows is the covenant of peace and the vow of marriage (2.19f.). A covenant is enacted containing all that man could possibly desire:

> In that day I will answer, says Yahweh,
> I will answer the heavens,
> and they will answer the earth,
> and the earth will answer the grain,
> the new wine, and the oil,
> and they will answer Jezreel (Hos. 2.21–22).

Thus the blood-guilt is washed away (cf. 1.4), the covenant of

grace is in force, and the people and God can only address each
other in one way, as 'my God' and 'my people' (2.23).

People were also convinced in Jerusalem that the wealth of Samaria
was the 'hire of a harlot' (Micah 1.7), but apart from this jibe little
reference is made to the myth of the *hieros gamos* by the Judean
prophets in the eighth century. A hundred years later, however, the
concept has gained currency; Jeremiah, too, describes the relationship between Yahweh and Israel as a failed marriage, probably
because he was familiar with the prophecies of Hosea. According
to him, the marriage began ideally:

> I (Yahweh) recall the faithfulness of your youth,
> your love as a bride,
> how you followed me in the wilderness,
> in the land that was unsown (Jer. 2.2).

Subsequently, however, things began to change. Israel deserted the
love of her youth and made the land, the 'orchard', unclean (v.7).
The people protest to no avail:

> I am not defiled,
> I have not gone after the Ba'als (v. 23).

But Jeremiah knows the extent of their flirtation with the Ba'als in
considerable detail:

> She went up on every high hill
> and under every green tree,
> and there played the harlot (3.6). . .
> They say to the tree, 'You are my father',
> and to the stone, 'You are my mother',[37]
> they turn their backs to me, not their faces (Jer. 2.27).

In Jeremiah's day the Northern Kingdom is a thing of the past,
and he fears that the Southern Kingdom could suffer a similar fate
at any moment. Therefore the prophet plays on the marriage metaphor so that Yahweh now has *two* unfaithful wives, and it is implied
that the example of the fate of the first wife should have a salutary
effect on the conduct of the second. Unfortunately, it does not.

This theme emerges from Jeremiah's parable of the two sisters,
mᵉšūbā and *bōgēdā* (or *bāgēdā*) (3.6ff.). First the elder sister turned
away (3.6) – her name means 'apostasy' – and accordingly received
a letter of divorce from her husband (3.8). Nor did the younger
sister, who was married to the same man, learn from her sister's

sad example: 'she too went and played the harlot' (3.8); indeed, she
behaved worse than her sister had done. Her name signifies 'faith-
lessness', which the prophet regards as worse than apostasy. Since
the younger sister had learnt nothing from her sister's example, the
parable concludes:

> *M^ešūbā* (Israel) is more righteous
> than *Bōgēdā*) (Judah) (Jer. 3.11).

Ezekiel recounts the same events in even clearer contours in ch.
23, where he discourses in some detail on the two sisters, *'Oh^olāh*
and *'Oh^olībāh*, [38] Samaria and Jerusalem. The erotic motifs of the
myth of the *hieros gamos* are here presented in no uncertain terms:
no one should be in any doubt how repugnant apostasy from Yahweh really is.

The same can be said of Ezek. 16, though in this case the subject
of discussion is Yahweh's adoptive child and lover, Jerusalem.
Nothing is left to the reader's imagination in this chapter; the
important thing seems to be that we should recognize sin for what
it is, and to label it accordingly. If we ignore the external form of
the passage, we immediately discover that the theme of the text is
an old acquaintance. It was Yahweh himself who had decked his
chosen one with finery (Ezek. 16.9ff.), while she was yet a helpless
infant (vv. 3ff.); however, maturing:

> You (Jerusalem) trusted in your beauty
> and played the harlot because of your renown (v. 15).

The good gifts of Yahweh came to be employed in the worship of
other gods (vv. 16ff.), and subsequently things went from bad to
worse:

> So I will judge you according to the law
> on whores and murderesses;
> I shall abandon you (?) to wrath and jealousy (v. 38).

But the judgment, which is depicted as the destruction of the city,
is hardly the last word in the relationship between Yahweh on the
one hand and Jerusalem and the people on the other:

> I will recall[39] my covenant with you
> – the one from the days of your youth –
> yes, I will make an eternal covenant with you.
> You will acknowledge your conduct and be ashamed (Ezek.
> 16.60f.).[40]

From royal ideology to messianism

King and temple play a rather central role in the Jerusalemite form of Yahwism; the temple, according to this ideology, has been built by the king and moreover, Yahweh is able to bring unruly vassals to heel merely by saying:

> I have set *my king* on Zion,
> my holy mountain (Ps. 2.6; see pp. 74f. and 83ff. above).

We should naturally expect to find that these associations are of limited importance among the prophets of the Northern Kingdom, Amos and Hosea. Admittedly, the book of Amos is introduced by a sort of epigram linking Yahweh to Jerusalem:

> Yahweh roars from Zion,
> and utters his voice from Jerusalem [41] (Amos 1.2).

Also, there are suggestions in both prophetic books of the notion that, when once judgment has been effected to the full, the true Israel will live in a unified state with a single – Davidic – monarch:

> Afterward the children of Israel will return,
> and seek Yahweh, their God, and David, their king (Hos. 3.5).[42]

But with the exceptions of these and a few similar references, we must look to the other prophets to find myths concerning the royal line and the temple.

Although it seems that the tradition of a dying and rising Ba'al (or Yahweh) who marries his consort Anath (see above, p. 77) was never a feature of the Jerusalem cult, corresponding notions concerning the earthly king did get a foothold. Kings of the house of David appropriated a number of 'Ba'al functions' connected with fertility and righteousness from Canaanite kingship (see p. 86). Thus a number of psalms, such as 18 and 89, can best be understood as expressing the cultic suffering and salvation of the king (see p. 88 and p. 133 n. 67). The prophets were also familiar with these rites and myths, even if they do not play any very significant part in the prophetic literature. Those passages which speak most forcefully of the fall of the divine king are concerned with foreign monarchs: the king of Babel (Isa. 14) and of Tyre (Ezek. 28). There are also various hints of the cultic suffering of the king in, for example, Micah 5.1, where the king's enemies strike him, 'Israel's judge', on the cheek with a staff (see p. 133 n. 70).

Further, if we accept the notion that the Suffering Servant poems of Deutero-Isaiah are texts of the royal cult, Isa. 53 must then be read as an expression of the myth of the suffering, death, resurrection, and justification of the king.[43] However, this interpretation is a bit too simplistic, however much truth it may contain. The servant of the poems bears evidence of characteristics which can be detected earlier on in the prophetic movement; unmerited suffering was, for example, the fate of Jeremiah, and Ezekiel demonstrates that a prophet can very well 'bear the people's burden of sin' (Ezek. 4.6).

The significance the Israelites saw in the birth of a royal heir shows that the marriage of the king and queen was regarded as so sacral in nature that it is not inappropriate to speak of the *hieros gamos* myth in this connection. Thus at a critical period in the history of Jerusalem, when the kings of Samaria and Damascus are attempting to compel King Ahaz into their anti-Assyrian coalition (at some point in the 730s), Isaiah presents himself to the king to offer first reassurance, and then threats, to make him refrain from joining (Isa. 7.1ff.). The prophet supports his contention that Ahaz has reason to believe in Yahweh's desire to save with the famous words:

> The young woman is with child,
> and she shall bear a son,
> and give him the name Immanuel (Isa. 7.14)

The young woman (*'almāh*) in question is probably the queen in her capacity as divine wife of the divine king; the entire prophecy may thus be seen as a reference to the myths of the sacred wedding. There is also a Canaanite parallel which supports this reading.[44]

It is of course vital to the survival of the dynasty that the queen should produce an heir to the throne; until this occurs the entire future is uncertain. Accordingly, the crucial period preceding the birth of an heir could be regarded as an expression of Yahweh's wrath:

> He will abandon them until the time
> when the woman in labour has given birth;
> then will the rest of his brothers
> return to the Israelites (Micah 5.3).

The expression 'the woman in labour' (*yōlēdāh*; lit. the 'birth-giver') is drawn from the vocabulary of myth; an equivalent expression is, among other things, used of Ishtar to express her qualities as mother goddess; and there is emphasis on those qualities which have to do with fertility rites and cultic prostitution.[45] In biblical language this concept leads to the metaphor of the birth pangs of the woman in labour; it signifies the horrors which are visited upon individuals (as in Isa. 13.8 and Jer. 6.24), or upon personified cities like Jerusalem (Micah 4.9f.) during the throes of the battle with chaos. Even Yahweh can feel like a woman in labour as he strives to achieve the salvation of Israel (Isa. 42.14). When the child who is to be king is born, it is an occasion of joy and expectation; his birth implies peace and ultimately victory, even over great powers like Assyria (Micah 5.4ff.):

> A child is born to us,
> a son is given to us;
> he has a ruler's mark on his shoulder
> and he is called 'Wonderful counsellor',
> 'God of heroes', 'Everlasting father',
> 'Prince of good fortune' (Isa. 9.6).

The names bestowed upon the royal offspring contain all Israel's hopes for the future: when the time comes for him to be anointed he receives the gift of Yahweh's spirit:

> . . . the spirit that is wisdom and understanding,
> that is counsel and might,
> that is knowledge (of Yahweh) and fear of Yahweh (Isa. 11.2).

Moreover, during his reign righteousness will be supreme in the world of men (Isa. 11.3–5), and paradisal harmony will prevail among the animals (Isa. 11.6–8):

> There is no one who does ill or does harm
> anywhere in all my holy mountain;
> for the earth is filled with the knowledge of Yahweh,
> as water covers the bottom of the sea (Isa. 11.9).

Indeed, in the cult texts of the royal temple, the king is everything he is ideally supposed to be (see p. 86). The prophets are quite lavish in their use of these texts since they have nothing against a monarch who is righteous and whose benevolent activity is present in all spheres of life:

> The king rules in righteousness,
> regents rule in justice,
> each of them is as shelter against the wind,
> and protection from the rain,
> like culverts in the desert,
> like the shadow of a great rock
> in the land of the thirsty (Isa. 32.1f.).

On the other hand, the ideal of righteousness often furnishes the prophets with criticisms of the reigning monarch.. The fact that Isaiah refers to the birth of the royal heir and emphasizes the blessings that will flow from it has much to do with the fact that Ahaz did not follow Isaiah's advice; his fear forced him to choose Assyrian aid and outweighed his ability to believe in aid from Yahweh.

It became customary for the prophets, when things were looking black for Israel, to refer to a future king. Thus, when Yahweh has done with punishing his people, things will return to normal:

> In those days at that time I will allow
> from (the line of) David a righteous branch
> to spring forth, which will obtain righteousness
> and justice in the land (Jer. 33.15; cf. 23.5).

When the 'dead' people have been revived, and the divided kingdom restored,

> then will my servant David be king over them –
> there shall be one shepherd for all of them!
> They shall follow my laws,
> and they shall keep my commandments
> and carry them out (Ezek. 37.24).

It is clear that after the return from their Babylonian captivity the people harbour certain expectations concerning a certain 'Branch from Babylon', Zerubbabel of David's line (e.g. Hagg. 2.23). We do not know what became of him. Perhaps he failed to live up to expectations; in any event, Zerubbabel disappears from history and the expectation of a future 'branch' from the tribe of David became a thing of the far future and is preserved in messianism. That which was originally set in the future in a polemic situation in order to save the divine but earthly kingdom became the foundation of the concept of a divine kingdom of heavenly origin.

Zion

When Yahweh has wiped away the sin of the people (Isa. 4.1ff.; see p. 101) and the right king reigns (Isa. 11.1–10; see p. 115), peace and security will prevail in Zion. The background of this tradition is the cultic drama of the battle for Jerusalem. The city will be the scene of various disasters before peace can reign:

> The palace is forsaken and the citizens abandoned,

Ophel and the watch tower are in ruins for ever (?),
for the enjoyment of wild asses, and pasture for cattle (Isa.
32.14; cf. Micah 3.12).

The only possible resolution of this unfortunate condition occurs when 'the spirit is poured upon us from on high' (Isa. 32.15).

It is one of Isaiah's cardinal themes that Jerusalem, or at any rate Zion, shall be saved in one way or another, even if a very grave situation arises first. When the king of Assyria, who as Isaiah admits has been sent against Israel as the vehicle of Yahweh's wrath ('the rod of my anger', Isa. 10.5), in his arrogance begins to imagine that Jerusalem will fall because of his own merits, he is told that the mountain of Zion is the place where Yahweh alone 'finishes all his work' (Isa. 10.12). This is the judging and saving activity of the cultic drama (cf. Pss. 46.8; 48.8f.; see p. 65f.).

While Isaiah seems to have hesitated to introduce the theme of the destruction of the temple unambiguously into the tradition, Jeremiah and Ezekiel, active a century later, were not so reticent. According to them, the people are not serious in their worship of God, and therefore:

I (Yahweh) will do to this house,
which is called by my name, in which you trust,
to the place which I gave to you and your fathers,
just as I did to Shiloh (Jer. 7.14).[46]

I will make this city a curse for all the nations of the earth
(Jer. 26.6).

And, of course, this is what happened in 587 when the Babylonians attacked the city: the temple was reduced to ruins. However, it is precisely because the destruction of the temple is part of a myth which has realized itself in history that the catastrophe does not imply that all is lost. Besides the despairing 'there may yet be hope' of Lamentations (3.29; see p. 93), the OT offers an alternative interpretation of the disaster. Ezekiel proclaims among the exiles that Israel's 'dead' shall live again (ch. 37; see p. 106f.), and he experiences in a vision the way the rebuilt temple is to look (Ezek. 40 ff.). Later, when it looks as if the Persian king Cyrus may be the anointed of the Lord who is to ensure Israel's return (Isa. 45.1 ff.), the proclamation of Deutero-Isaiah is one of 'good tidings to Zion' (Isa. 40.9).

All this expresses the belief that the temple is the centre of the world, identified with the mountain of the gods in the north (Ps.

48.2).[47] It is an ancient idea that at the time of salvation Zion, as the highest mountain on earth, will attract the whole world to her feet (Isa. 2.2; Micah 4.1); this theme was preserved among the prophets until prophecy in its typical form died out and was replaced by apocalyptic.

> Then will all the survivors of all peoples
> who come to Jerusalem
> go up year after year
> to worship the King, Yahweh of Hosts,
> and keep the Feast of Booths.
> But if any of the races of the earth do not go up
> to Jerusalem to worship the King, Yahweh of Hosts,
> no rain will fall upon them (Zech. 14.16f.).[48]

Other motifs of the myth of the New Year Festival

The catastrophes which, according to the prophets, could strike down Jerusalem and the temple can be described in the language of the myth of the battle with the nations (see pp. 72ff.).

The prophet *Joel*, whose activities are difficult to date with certainty, describes a particular misfortune, a plague of grasshoppers, as a hostile attack (or is it perhaps vice versa?). Famine is one of the consequences of the plague; Joel interprets it as punishment from Yahweh. On this occasion, the people save themselves by repenting. After their lament Yahweh reverses the situation, so that the people have food again:

> I (Yahweh) will send to you grain, new wine, and oil,
> and you will be satisfied with it,
> and I will not again make you
> an outrage among the peoples.
> I will expel the northerner from you,
> and drive him into a parched and desolate land (Joel 2.19f.)

The spirit is poured out over the people (Joel 2.28ff.), while their enemies are gathered together for judgment (3.1ff); all the people of Israel participate in the judgment as warriors (3.10f.),[49] and the harmonious relationship between Yahweh and the people is re-established:

> Yahweh roars from Zion
> and from Jerusalem he raises up his voice
> so that heaven and earth tremble.
> But Yahweh is a refuge for his people,

a bulwark for the Israelites.
So you shall know that I am Yahweh, your God,
who dwells on Zion, my holy mountain;
Jerusalem will be holy,
and no strangers will ever storm it again (Joel 3.16f.).

Jeremiah understands the threat from the north in concrete historical terms, as referring to the turmoil among the great political and military powers which spelled the beginning of the end of Assyrian dominance in the Near East. This is stated in connection with Jeremiah's call-vision, as an interpretation of an otherwise natural event, the boiling over of a pot whose contents then run down from the north:

Evil will erupt from the north
against all those dwelling in the land.
For behold, says Yahweh, I will call upon
all the races of the northern kingdoms,
and they will come, and each will raise up his throne
before the gates of Jerusalem,
against all its walls round about,
and against all the cities of Judah (Jer. 1.14f.).

This is a typical example of the process by which myth becomes history; an equally typical example is to be found in Isa. 7–8. After King Ahaz has rejected Isaiah's admonitions and asked the Assyrians for help against the kings of Samaria and Damascus, the prophet maintains that Yahweh will visit punishment upon the land in the form of Assyrian attack. The people are to be punished for their lack of faith in Yahweh, which is epitomized by their lack of confidence in their water supplies, which come from the sacred spring and along the rock-cut channel of Siloam (Isa. 8.6):

Therefore the Lord will let the great and mighty waters
of the river rise up against them:
the king of Assyria in all his glory.
It will well up over all its channels,
and run over all its banks,
and go over Judah,
it will flood and advance
until it reaches the neck.
But his wide open arms will
fill the entire country (Isa. 8.7f.).

However, the text continues with a warning to the invaders not to go too far; they have no possibility of realizing their own plans:

Be assembled, you people, and be afraid:
listen well, all you far countries.
Gird yourselves and be afraid,
gird yourselves and be afraid.
Make a plan, but it will collapse;
discuss an issue, though it will fall (Isa. 8.9f.).

Both these texts indicate unambiguously that the real subject of
historical activity is Yahweh, who is part and parcel of the devel-
opments. He will indeed punish his own people, but he will not
omit to reveal to the heathen who it is that has given them permis-
sion to wage war. Thus in one of the Zion Psalms after the conclusion of the battle with the nations we read:

Be still and know that I am God,
exalted among the peoples,
exalted in the earth (Ps. 46.10.)

The relationship of Isaiah's thought to that of Ps. 46 is apparent at
another point:

Yahweh of Hosts is *with us*;
our bulwark is the God of Jacob (Ps. 46.7,11).

This is the refrain of the psalm, and must be considered an established expression of the cult. Both Isa. 8.8 and 8.10 play on this
cultic usage, since both the conclusion of the depiction of the battle
and the conclusion of the warning to the heathen end with the royal
name, Immanuel, which as we know means 'with us God'.[50]

God is thus seen as being present in misfortune as well as good
times. When the people sin, he brings disaster upon them, but by
the same token they are fortunate that he is with them when the
catastrophe strikes.

In the prophetic literature, prophecies of both doom and salvation
are often introduced by the expression *bayyōm hahū'*, 'in that day'.
It is clear from Isa. 2.11–12 that it is quite a special day that
Yahweh has had assigned to himself; it is the day on which all of
the forces of creation are mobilized against whatever opposes Yahweh (Isa. 2.12ff.); it is the festival day, New Year's Day, the time
of the theophany of Yahweh (see pp. 79ff.). Naturally enough, the
day of Yahweh is often the day of Yahweh's triumph over the
foreign nations (Isa. 13.6,9; Ezek. 30.3; Joel 2.32, etc.). However,
the day is not always necessarily a bright one for Israel; when the
people have sinned, the day of Yahweh is darkness. It is therefore

characteristic that the book of Joel assigns to the day of Yahweh not only the divine vengeance upon Israel's enemies, but also the plague itself:

> Alas for the day! The day of Yahweh is near,
> it comes bearing destruction (Joel 1.15).[51]

Similarly, when Ezekiel proclaims judgment before the fall of Jerusalem, he is able to focus his description of the coming adversities by use of the expression 'the day of the wrath of the Lord' (Ezek. 7.19). Also, after the great misfortune has occurred, the author of Lamentations likewise depicts this day of wrath in the most frightening manner imaginable (Lam. 2).

Ultimately, however, there is no doubt at all of the prophets' conviction that the last day of Yahweh, or rather, the last act of Yahweh on his day, would entail the final victory over the enemies of God and his people.[52]

In the prophetic interpretation of the Hebrew corpus of myths it was often possible to distribute the tension between judgment and salvation along a line of historical process; nevertheless, it is not to be denied that the transition between the two phases sometimes seems to be somewhat abrupt. For this reason, the prophets sought various means of reducing the intensity of this apparent contradiction. One of these was the concept of the *remnant*. It is conceivable that the 'remnant' was originally a cultic term for the Israel which would survive after the battle with the nations:

> Every one who calls on Yahweh's name will be saved,
> for on Zion's mountain and in Jerusalem there will be rescue
> – Yahweh has spoken thus! –
> and every one Yahweh calls will belong to the remnant (Joel 2.32).

We should observe that a problem arises as soon as the judgment is directed internally, against Israel, since we cannot without more ado identify the remnant with Israel as a whole.

Isaiah in particular attempts to solve this problem. One of his sons is named Shear-Jashub, 'a remnant shall return' (Isa. 7.3). Like Immanuel, this name conveys both a threat and a promise. To those who fail to take the reality of the judgment seriously it becomes a threat: *only* a remnant shall return. To those who accept the fact that judgment is Yahweh's only possible means of securing a people who will live within the framework of his covenant, then the phrase bears the promise that, come what may, a remnant *shall* return.

The double-sided conception of Yahweh as Creator and King underlies the whole of the prophetic proclamation. In what we have said above, this idea has been evident several times in the way Yahweh has been described. The descriptions of the mythology of creation which appear in the previous chapters of this work are also applicable to prophetism; further, the prophetic literature can hardly give a more accurate impression of the Israelite understanding of creation than that which we encounter in Genesis and the Psalms. It was of decisive importance for the prophets that their contemporaries should understand creation not only as a past event, but also as a present reality. For this reason we find that they frequently employ the creation myths in the context of a concrete historical situation.

Deutero-Isaiah offers a textbook example of this procedure in Isa. 51.9 ff. After the introductory challenge to Yahweh to awake (see p. 104), the prophet employs the motif of the battle with the dragon, which is one of the figures of the myth of creation:

> For it was you who clove Rahab,
> who pierced the dragon (Isa. 51.9).

This is then interpreted in the following exodus myth, which is of course one of the myths fundamental to Israel's understanding of her origin and election (see pp. 69ff.):

> For it was you who dried up the sea (*yām*),
> the waters of the great deep (*tᵉhōm*)
> who made (?) the deeps into a path
> which the redeemed trod upon (Isa. 51.10).

The exodus myth is subsequently actualized by the prophet, who applies it to the event for which he longs, the return from Babylon:

> The ransomed of Yahweh shall return;
> they will enter Zion with jubilation (Isa. 51.11).[53]

This way of editing the mythical materials is quite natural for Deutero-Isaiah (cf. e.g. Isa. 43.14ff.) and the other prophets.

In retrospect, we should observe that the prophets' choice of themes was not especially original; on the other hand, they possessed a remarkable ability to choose the theme most appropriate to a given situation. Myths thus function in prophetic language in such an integral way that it is impossible to separate them out as a foreign element. Nor do the prophets utilize myth to promulgate dogmatic or historical truths about Yahweh, or to describe his nature and will, but from one situation to another to communicate the truth of the relationship between Yahweh and Israel.

NOTES

1 The Concept of Myth

1. On myth research and the critical evaluation of myth during the Enlightenment and the Romantic period, see C. Hartlich and W. Sachs, *Der Ursprung des Mythosbegriffes*, Tübingen 1952, and J. W. Rogerson, *Myth in Old Testament Interpretation*, BZAW 134, 1974. See also K. Ruthven, *Myth*, Methuen and Barnes & Noble, New York 1976, pp. 5–17.

2. P. G. Lindhardt, *Grundtvig: An Introduction*, Copenhagen 1951, esp. pp. 14–16 on Grundtvig's understanding of Schelling and his view of myth. Cf. also E. L. Allen, *Bishop Grundtvig: A Prophet of the North*, James Clarke 1949.

3. E. Buess, *Die Geschichte des mythischen Erkennens*, Munich 1953, pp. 93ff.

4. H. W. Bartsch (ed.), *Kerygma and Myth*, ET SPCK 1953, p. 10 (here quoted from B. S. Childs, *Myth and Reality in the Old Testament*, SBT 1.27, 1968, p. 14, and Rogerson, op. cit., p. 155).

5. N. F. S. Grundtvig, *Krønnike-Rim til levende Skolebrug* (1842), Copenhagen [3]1875, p. 263.

6. A. Olrik, *Nogle Grundsaetninger for Sagnforskning*, Copenhagen 1921, p. 36.

7. H. Gunkel, *Genesis*, HAT 1, [5]1922, p. xiv; it should be mentioned that Gunkel frequently refers to Olrik's work (above). Gunkel's understanding of myth has found its way in innumerable places into the critical literature on the OT. See e.g. Otto Eissfeldt's standard work, *Introduction to the Old Testament*, ET Blackwell, Oxford, and Harper & Row, New York 1965, p. 35. For criticism of Gunkel's definition see e.g. Childs, *Myth and Reality*, pp. 15f.

8. G. van der Leeuw, *Religion in Essence and Manifestation*, ET Macmillan 1938, pp. 413–17; J. Sløk, 'Mythos I. Begrifflich und Religionspsychologisch', *RGG*[3] IV, 1960, cols. 1263–8. For additional literature on the contemporary discussion of myth see Childs, op. cit., p. 17 n. 1.

9. Olrik, op. cit., p. 33.

10. C.-M. Edsman, 'Sagen und Legenden I. Allgemeines', *RGG*[3] V, 1961, col. 1300; cf. Sløk, op. cit., col. 1263.

11. Cf. B. O. Long, *The Problem of Etiological Narrative in the Old Testament*, BZAW 108, 1968.

12. Sløk, op. cit., col. 1263.

13. K. Koch, *The Growth of the Biblical Tradition*, ET A. & C. Black and Scribner's, New York 1969, pp. 111–32.

14. Van der Leeuw, op. cit., p. 414; Sløk, op. cit., col. 1263.

15. Of Mircea Eliade's many works I should like to call attention to two in particular: *The Sacred and the Profane*, ET Harcourt, Brace & World, New York 1959, and *The Myth of the Eternal Return*, ET Routledge & Kegan Paul and Pantheon Press, New York 1955, reissued Princeton University Press 1971.

16. Eliade, *Sacred and Profane*, pp. 91f.; on the two conceptions of time see pp. 68ff., 104f., and Childs, *Myth and Reality*, pp. 73–5.

17. S. Mowinckel, *Religion og Kultus*, Oslo 1950, pp. 65–8; in *The Myth of the Eternal Return*, ch. 2, 'The Regeneration of Time', Eliade offers a collection of examples drawn from cultures as widely divergent as possible, in illustration of the significance man has accorded the coming of the New Year.

18. V. Grønbech, *Illustreret Religionshistorie*, Copenhagen ²1948, pp. 56f.; see the entire section on primitive cultus, pp. 54–73. For the copious recent literature on the nature of the cult see e.g. G. Widengren, *Religionsphänomenologie*, Berlin 1969, pp. 209–57; Mowinckel, op. cit., pp. 50–75.

19. Widengren, op. cit., pp. 150 and 174f.; cf. also the classical formulation by S. H. Hooke in 'The Myth and Ritual Pattern of the Ancient East' in the collection of essays edited by him, *Myth and Ritual*, OUP 1933, p. 3.

20. Mowinckel, op. cit., p. 79. Childs, *Myth and Reality*, pp. 19f., treats the relationship of myth and cult and refers to essential literature.

21. Kaj Thaning, *Menneske først . . .*, Copenhagen 1963, p. 284, with a reference to *Nordens Mythologi*, 1832 (Udv. Skrifter ved Begtrup, vol. 5, p. 675).

22. Sløk, op. cit., col. 1263; also Childs, op. cit., pp. 18–21, strongly emphasizing this aspect of myth. Cf. James Barr, 'The Meaning of Mythology', *VT* 9, 1959, p. 3: 'Mythology is . . . a serious attempt at integration of reality and experience.'

23. Grønbech, op. cit., p. 60.

24. Eliade, *Sacred and Profane*, pp. 95–97.

25. F. Heiler, *Erscheinungsformen und Wesen der Religion*, Stuttgart 1961, pp. 283–6.

26. Both Widengren (op. cit., pp. 244f.) and Childs (op. cit., pp. 26f.) offer the Babylonian creation narrative as an important example. Cf. the excellent treatment of the whole epic by Thorkild Jacobsen in *The Treasures of Darkness*, Yale University Press 1976, pp. 167–91.

27. *ANET*, p. 67.

28. *ANET*, p. 68; cf. *NERT*, p. 84.

29. Eliade, *The Myth of the Eternal Return*, p. 56.

30. O. E. Ravn, *Illustreret Religionshistorie*, ²1948, p. 172.

31. *ANET*, pp. 64f. 70.

32. Eliade, *Eternal Return*, pp. 23–7, brings parallel examples from numerous religions. Cf. Widengren, op. cit., pp. 235–43.

33. Widengren, op. cit., pp. 159–61.

34. *Handbuch der Religionsgeschichte*, ed. J. P. Asmussen and J. Laessøe, vol.

2, Göttingen 1972, p. 48. Similarly A. Caquot, *Die Schöpfungsmythen*, Zürich and Cologne 1964, pp. 179–81. A. S. Kapelrud, *Baal in the Ras Shamra Texts*, Copenhagen 1952, p. 131, does not accept this idea.

35. Flemming Hvidberg, *Weeping and Laughter in the Old Testament* (posthumous English edition by Frede Løkkegaard, incorporating the results of later Ugaritic scholarship), Leiden: Brill, and Copenhagen 1962; these texts on pp. 22–40 (cf. *NERT*, pp. 213–20).

36. Ba'al's father, the corn god.

37. Johannes Pedersen, *Handbuch der Religionsgeschichte* 2, 1972, p. 41.

38. Pedersen, ibid., p. 47.

2 The Use of Myth in Genesis

1. Gerhard von Rad in particular has stressed this point; see 'Typological Interpretation of the Old Testament' in *Essays on Old Testament Interpretation*, ed. C. Westermann, ET SCM Press and John Knox Press, Richmond, Va. 1963, pp. 17–39; cf. Childs, *Myth and Reality*, p. 103.

2. G. von Rad, *Genesis*, ET, OTL, [3]1972, p. 152ff. (on the primeval history), and J. Pedersen, *Israel* I–II, ET Copenhagen and OUP 1926, p. 190 (on the patriarchal sagas).

3. G. Widengren, 'Hebrew Myths and their Interpretation' in *Myth, Ritual and Kingship*, ed. S. H. Hooke, OUP 1958, pp. 158f., 200–02; quotation from p. 201; a similar view was suggested earlier by Pedersen, *Israel* I–II, p. 471.

4. Von Rad, *Genesis*, p. 50. A similar view has been voiced in Scandinavian circles by G. Gerleman, 'Gamla testament och mytologien', *Aktuella problem i gammaltestamentlig forskning*, Fällköping 1971, p. 14.

5. K. I. Johannesen, 'Innledning til Første Mosebok' in *Første Mosebok: En kommentar*, ed. A. Bjørndalen, Oslo 1970, p. 32; cf. also p. 36, where he proposes alternative typologies of the stories in Genesis.

6. W. H. Schmidt, *Alttestamentlicher Glaube und sein Umwelt*, Neukirchen 1968, pp. 158f.; 'Mythos im Alten Testament', *EvTh* 27, 1967, p. 249; cf. Gerleman, op. cit., pp. 14–16.

7. Pedersen, *Israel* I–II, p. 471.

8. See e.g. in *IDB Suppl* the articles on 'Biblical Criticism: OT' (Cazelles); 'Tradition Criticism, OT' (Coats); 'Yahwist' (Brueggemann); 'Priestly Writers' (Levine); 'Deuteronomy' (Lohfink), etc. See also the many modern Introductions to the OT, most of which are available in English, e.g. those of Bentzen (1949), Weiser (1961), Eissfeldt (1965) and Soggin (1976); also Ivan Engnell, 'The Pentateuch' in *A Rigid Scrutiny: Critical Essays on the Old Testament*, ET Abingdon Press, Nashville 1969 (= *Critical Essays . . .*, SPCK 1970), pp. 50–67.

9. Cf. B. Otzen, '*bādal*', *TDOT* II, pp. 1–3; on the use of the word specifically in Genesis see W. H. Schmidt, *Die Schöpfungsgeschichte der Priesterschrift*, Neukirchen 1967, p. 167; cf. this view with that of M. Saebø, 'Creator et Redemptor', *Deus Creator: Bidrag til Skabelsesteologien*, Festschrift for I. P. Seierstad, Oslo 1971, pp. 19f., which strongly emphasizes the elements from the Wisdom tradition in Gen. 1.

10. A. Bjørndalen, 'Om syntaks, stil og mening i Genesis 1.1–3a', *Deus Creator . . .*, pp. 39–43, discussing the views of Westermann and W. H. Schmidt on the relationship between tradition and interpretation in Genesis; cf. also Westermann, *Genesis*, BKAT I,1, 1966, pp. 113ff.

11. Schmidt, op. cit., p. 161. Certain problems in Schmidt's translation will be touched upon below.

12. H. Gunkel, *Genesis*, HAT ⁵1922, p. 118.

13. Paul Humbert, 'La relation de Genése 1 et du Psaume 104 avec la liturgie du Nouvel-An israëlite', *RHPR* 15, 1935, pp. 1–27.

14. H. Ringgren, 'Är den bibliska skapelseberättelsen en kulttext?', *SEÅ* 13, 1948, pp. 9–21.

15. Eduard Nielsen, 'Skal vi have en ny oversaettelse af Det Gamle Testamente' (art. publ. by Det danske Bibelselskab [the Danish Bible Society] in 1971), p. 6; cf. von Rad, *Genesis*, pp. 49–51; Humbert, 'Trois notes sur Gen. 1', *Interpretationes Veteris Testamenti S. Mowinckel* (= *NTT* 56), 1955, pp. 85–8; cf. also Bjørndalen's contribution, n. 10 above, and the discussion of the two possibilities of translation by Childs, *Myth and Reality*, pp. 31ff.; on p. 40 Childs argues for the traditional translation. Cf. also Westermann, *Genesis*, pp. 130–35.

16. *ANET*, pp. 60f.; cf. *NERT*, p. 82.

17. On Apsu, see pp. 13f.; Kulla is the 'brick-god'; our text is taken from A. Heidel, *The Babylonian Genesis*, University of Chicago Press 1963, p. 65; on pp. 61–81 Heidel lists a number of Babylonian parallels to the *Enuma Elish* and discusses the introductory formula mentioned here.

18. Westermann, *Genesis*, p. 141: 'For P it is not the depictions of chaos as such that matter, but rather the antithesis.'

19. Pedersen, *Israel* I–II, pp. 456f.

20. Ibid., pp. 464–6.

21. Bjørndalen, *Deus Creator*, pp. 44f.; cf. Childs, *Myth and Reality*, pp. 36f.

22. Gunkel, *Genesis*, p. 104.

23. See n. 15 and Ringgren, *SEÅ* 13, 1948, pp. 15f.

24. Again, Schmidt, *Schöpfungsgeschichte*, p. 83; he points out that the corresponding verb in Ugaritic means simply 'to fly'.

25. D. Winton Thomas, 'Some Unusual Ways of Expressing the Superlative in Hebrew', *VT* 3, 1953, p. 210; Schmidt, op. cit., p. 84.

26. Schmidt, op. cit., p. 86.

27. Pedersen, *Israel* I–II, p. 470.

28. Ibid., p. 457; von Rad, *Genesis*, pp. 50f.; Childs, *Myth and Reality*, p. 43.

29. Pedersen, *Israel* I–II, pp. 459f.; Childs, loc. cit.

30. Von Rad, *Genesis*, pp. 51f.

31. On vv. 11–12 see von Rad, ibid., pp. 54f.; on v. 21 see Schmidt, op. cit., p. 122; see also the note on the dragon motif, Childs, op. cit., p. 38.

32. Von Rad, *Genesis*, pp. 76f.

33. Heidel, *Babylonian Genesis*, p. 62; cf. also Bjørndalen, *Første Mosebok*, pp. 55–8.

34. *Enuma Elish* VI. 33ff.: *ANET*, p. 68; cf. *NERT*, p. 61, and Heidel,

Babylonian Genesis, pp. 69f. (text from Assur).

35. Schmidt, op. cit., p. 198; text: *ANET*, p. 425 (Instruction of Amen-ʿm-ʿopet); cf. *NERT*, p. 61.

36. *ANET*, p. 74.

37. Heidel, *Babylonian Genesis*, pp. 65f.

38. Ibid., p. 67.

39. Ibid., p. 78.

40. A similar idea is to be found in the notion of the '*imago Dei*' in Gen. 1.26; cf. Schmidt, op. cit., pp. 127–49.

41. Epic of Gilgamesh: *ANET*, pp. 72ff.; Adapa: *ANET*, pp. 101–3; full treatment of the Gilgamesh epic now by Thorkild Jacobsen in *Treasures of Darkness*, Yale University Press 1976, pp. 195–219.

42. *ANET*, p. 96.

43. See e.g. Ringgren, *SBU* II, 1963, p. 430; Childs, *Myth and Reality*, pp. 46–8.

44. F. Hvidberg, 'The Canaanite Background of Genesis I–III', *VT* 10, 1960, pp. 285–94.

45. Tenth song of the Gilgamesh epic: *ANET*, p. 90; cf. Westermann, *Genesis*, p. 292.

46. Westermann, op. cit., p. 337; on pp. 330–33 he presents a convenient list of diverging views on the tree of knowledge, of which the more important are mentioned here. See also the commentaries for additional information.

47. Gunkel, *Genesis*, pp. 17f.; von Rad, *Genesis*, p. 91.

48. I. Engnell, ' "Knowledge" and "Life" in the Creation Story', in *Wisdom in Israel*, SVT 3, 1960, pp. 103–19, esp. pp. 114–16.

49. Ibid., p. 116.

50. James Barr, 'The Meaning of "Mythology" in Relation to the Old Testament', *VT* 9, 1959, pp. 1–10.

51. Pedersen, *Israel* I–II, p. 470.

52. Sverre Aalen, 'Kosmos og kaos i bibelsk taenking', in *Deus Creator*, p. 58: 'Man finds himself leading an existence threatened by powers with which he cannot cope, but which also create a *modus vivendi* for him. This brings in its train conflict, difficulty and danger.' Remarkably, Aalen asserts that the biblical concept does not entail the view that this state of affairs only came about after the fall.

53. Von Rad, *Genesis*, pp. 92f.

54. Pedersen, op. cit., p. 466.

55. If we assume that the narrative is seeking to express a dualism of this kind in agricultural life, it is unnecessary to follow von Rad (*Genesis*, p. 94) in postulating two interwoven versions, one that of the peasant (vv. 17 and 19ab), the other that of the bedūin (vv. 18 and 19c).

56. *ANET*, pp. 93–5; cf. *NERT*, pp. 93–7; in *The Gilgamesh Epic*, pp. 102–19, Heidel presents more or less fragmentary Sumerian and Babylonian parallels to the flood narrative of the Gilgamesh epic.

57. Heidel, *The Gilgamesh Epic*, p. 107.

58. Eduard Nielsen, *Oral Tradition*, ET, SBT 1.11, 1954, pp. 93–103.

59. S. H. Hooke, 'Cain and Abel', *Folk-lore* 50, London 1939, pp. 58–65; I. Engnell, 'Kain och Abel', *Svenska Jerusalemsföreningens Tidskrift* 46, Stock-

holm 1947, pp. 92–102.

60. Cf. von Rad, *Genesis*, p. 149; on Gen. 6. 1–4 see the commentaries and Childs, *Myth and Reality*, pp. 50–59.

61. Pedersen, *Israel* III–IV, pp. 749f.

62. Childs, op. cit., pp. 75–84, emphasizes the eschatological aspect of this development. Cf. also Barr, *VT* 9, 1959, pp. 9–10.

63. M. Saebø, op. cit. (see n. 9), p. 8.

64. Von Rad, *Old Testament Theology* I, ET Oliver & Boyd and Harper & Row, New York 1962, reissued SCM Press 1975, p. 139; Gerleman, op. cit. (see n. 4), pp. 14f.

3 Myth in the Psalms

1. The understanding of the Psalms here presented may be regarded as an extension of the fundamental work of the Norwegian scholar Sigmund Mowinckel, in his *Psalmenstudien* I–VI, Oslo 1921–24, and *The Psalms in Israel's Worship*, ET Abingdon, New York 1962, Blackwell, Oxford 1963 (quoted as *The Psalms*). For an excellent introduction to Psalm research as well as a balanced appraisal of Mowinckel's work, see the article on the Psalms by A. R. Johnson in *The Old Testament and Modern Study*, ed. H. H. Rowley, OUP 1951, pp. 162–209.

2. G. Widengren, *Religionsphänomenologie*, 1969, pp. 150ff.

3. S. H. Hooke, 'The Myth and Ritual Pattern of the Ancient East' in *Myth and Ritual*, ed. Hooke, OUP 1933, p. 1. The word 'ritual' in the quotation may be acceptably rendered 'cultic drama'. For the concept of myth see ch. 1 above. The definition employed here corresponds more or less to that of Mowinckel in 'Das Thronbesteigungsfest Jahwäs und der Ursprung der Eschatologie', *Psalmenstudien* II, p. 45 n. 1, and Widengren, op. cit., pp. 150–7.

4. This is the impression gained from F. F. Hvidberg, *Weeping and Laughter in the Old Testament*, ET 1962; cf. T. H. Gaster's use of the word 'libretti' in 'New Light on Early Palestinian Religion', *Religions* 18, London January 1937, pp. 7ff.

5. So e.g. I. Engnell, *Studies in Divine Kingship in the Ancient Near East*, Blackwell, Oxford [2]1967, pp. 97ff.

6. J. Laessøe, 'Babylonische und assyrische Religion' in J. P. Asmussen and J. Laessøe (eds.), *Handbuch der Religionsgeschichte* I, Göttingen 1971, pp. 520ff.

7. A. R. Johnson, *Sacral Kingship in Ancient Israel*, University of Wales Press, Cardiff [2]1967, p. 127.

8. Translation in *ANET*, pp. 331–4.

9. On Pss. 46.9; (66.5); 48.9f., see Mowinckel, *Psalmenstudien* II, pp. 126–8; H. Ringgren, *The Faith of the Psalmists*, ET SCM Press and Fortress Press, Philadelphia 1963, p. 161; Johnson, op. cit., pp. 87ff.

10. Cf. Ps. 44.2–4.

11. Cf. Johnson, op. cit., p. 88; E. Nielsen, 'Die Religion des alten Israel' in Asmussen and Laessøe, *Handbuch* II, p. 88. We are of course prepared to admit that the word may be translated 'think' (as in RSV).

12. Our point of departure here is Mowinckel, *Psalmenstudien* II, pp. 45–80; cf. *The Psalms* I, pp. 140–69; cf. also his translation of and notes to the Psalms in *Det Gamle Testamente* IV, Oslo 1955, pp. 25–292.

13. Ps. 104. 10–18 may be regarded as a continuation of the creation myth first adumbrated in vv. 5–9.

14. See references in ch. 1 n. 34 above.

15. This is the central thesis of Fritz Stolz's exciting work *Strukturen und Figuren im Kult von Jerusalem*, BZAW 118, 1970, p. 36.

16. For Marduk's curses in his battle with Tiamat, see A. Heidel, *The Babylonian Genesis*, 1942, p. 38.

17. The temple is called 'Yahweh's dwelling' in vv. 17f.; see also Mowinckel, *Psalmenstudien* II, p. 56; *The Psalms* I, p. 155.

18. Cf. Ringgren, *Faith of the Psalmists*, pp. 102ff.

19. The Egyptians did not speak Hebrew; cf. the original connotation of the Greek word *barbaros*, barbarian.

20. See B. Albrektson, *History and the Gods*, which is subtitled 'An Essay on the Idea of Historical Events as Divine Manifestations in the Ancient Near East and Israel', Lund 1967.

21. Ringgren, op. cit., pp. 198ff.

22. G. von Rad, the title essay in *The Problem of the Hexateuch*, ET Oliver & Boyd, Edinburgh and McGraw Hill, New York 1966, pp. 1–78; cf. A. Bentzen, *Introduction to the Old Testament* II, Gad, Copenhagen 1948, pp. 76ff.

23. Ringgren, op. cit., pp. 1–10.

24. According to Canaanite mythology the 'mountain of God' lay in the far north (Zaphon); see Isa. 14.13; cf. Ezek. 28.14ff. We meet the same idea in the texts from Ras Shamra-Ugarit, where Ba'al dwells on Zapan's mountain: 'This is not a geographical location, but it expresses the idea that the gods dwell at the navel of the world, and that this is to be located in the temple', J. Pedersen, 'Kanaanäische Religion' in Asmussen, *Handbuch* II, p. 47.

25. Mowinckel, *Psalmenstudien* II, p. 57–65; cf. *The Psalms* I, pp. 151–4.

26. See above, p. 66.

27. 'Moved', which is suggested by RSV, is not of course incorrect; in our translation, however, we have attempted to bring out the unity of the psalm by means of the verbs 'fall' and 'collapse' as renderings of the original Hebrew.

28. See e.g. C. A. and E. C. Briggs, *The Book of Psalms* I, ICC, 1906, pp. 393ff.

29. See the Hebrew account in II Kings 18.13 – 19.37 and the Akkadian in *ANET*, pp. 287f.

30. Stolz, *Strukturen und Figuren*, pp. 80–82; we should also note that Stolz is by no means the only advocate of a purely 'historical' interpretation. He feels that the motif of the battle with the nations was a traditional element of the hymnology of the cultic drama, in which the cultic myth was interpreted as the actual political reality.

31. Cf. e.g. the oracle in II Kings 19.21–34, in which the actual emergency of 701 BC is interpreted on the basis of an anthropological myth with

the motif of *hybris*.

32. In this connection we should note that it is the predicate 'by the grace of God' that is significant.

33. Johnson, *Sacral Kingship*, pp. 85ff.; Stolz, op. cit., pp. 86ff.

34. Stolz, ibid.

35. Quoted from A. Falkenstein and W. von Soden, *Sumerische und akkadische Hymnen und Gebete*, Zurich and Stuttgart 1953, p. 63; cf. Stolz, op. cit., p. 75. On pp. 75–85 Stolz gives a number of examples from Mesopotamia and Ugarit.

36. The 'good' shepherd' is, of course, the king.

37. Cf. the quotation from *Enuma Elish*, above, pp. 00f.

38. This objection has been raised by, among others, E. Auerbach, 'Neujahrs- und Versöhnungsfest in den biblischen Quellen', *VT* 8, 1958, pp. 337–41.

39. It was primarily a group of English scholars who first made use of a cultic pattern in the analysis of the New Year festivals which were celebrated in the ancient Near East. See S. H. Hooke (ed.), *Myth and Ritual*, OUP 1933, and *The Labyrinth*, SPCK and Macmillan, New York 1935. This 'patternism', as it has come to be called, has been taken further in Scandinavia thanks to the efforts of the Swedish scholars Widengren and Engnell in a long series of works on the Psalms. Although Mowinckel was critical of the way these two scholars developed their special variety of patternism, his own psalm research, in which he made extensive use of Akkadian material (e.g. in *Psalmenstudien* II) would have to be described as a distinguished example of patternism.

40. Widengren thinks that he has found reminiscences of the concept of the death of Yahweh in such formulae as 'Rouse yourself, O Lord! Why do you sleep?' (Pss. 44.23; cf. 35.23; 59.4b; 78.61, 65f.). See 'Early Hebrew Myths and their Interpretation' in Hooke (ed.), *Myth, Ritual and Kingship*, OUP 1958, pp. 191f.

41. The explanation offered here is to be found in Hvidberg, 'Tro og Moral', in *Håndbog i Kristendomskundskab* II, Copenhagen 1943, pp. 253–7; Mowinckel, *The Psalms* I, pp. 136–40.

42. Cf. Engnell, *Critical Essays*, pp. 25f.

43. Cf. Stolz, *Strukturen und Figuren*, p. 154.

44. So Mowinckel in the subtitle to *Psalmenstudien* II (cf. n. 3 above).

45. E. Hammershaimb, *Some Aspects of Old Testament Prophecy*, Copenhagen 1966, p. 77.

46. Quoted from Hvidberg, *Weeping and Laughter*, p. 48 (text II AB VII 28f); cf. *NERT*, p. 211.

47. On this point Stolz (op. cit., pp. 153f.) regards it as improbable that an Israelite who was reworking the text should, after borrowing this material directly from a Canaanite description of Ba'al, have then replaced Ba'al's name with the no less Canaanite epithet El Elyon.

48. Here we should perhaps, with W. F. Albright, read 'Lord of Sinai'. Cf. Albright, 'A Catalogue of Early Hebrew Lyric Poems', *HUCA* 23, 1950/51, p. 20.

49. H.-J. Kraus, *Psalmen*, BKAT, [2]1961, p. 203.

50. See above, pp. 63ff., and Ringgren, *Faith of the Psalmists*, pp. xvi–xviii.

51. Pedersen, *Israel* III–IV, pp. 229ff.

52. Mowinckel, *The Psalms* I, pp. 173–81.

53. I.e., Kiriath-Jearim.

54. A particular type of psalm.

55. Crucial for the understanding of the formula '*YHWH malak*', 'Yahweh has become king', is the fact that the same formula was used on the occasion of the enthronement of the earthly king. Thus in the succession narrative the new king is acknowledged with the shout 'Absalom has become king!' (II Sam. 15.10); similarly II Kings 9.13 reads: 'Jehu has become king!' Cf. Mowinckel, *Psalmenstudien* II, p. 6.

56. Cf. I Kings 6.1, 2, 12, 14, 21, etc.

57. This is made apparent by the precautions which, according to I Kings 12.26f., Jeroboam felt compelled to take after the division of the kingdom.

58. As Mowinckel thinks; see *The Psalms* I, pp. 70 and 224.

59. For the Israelite form of the common oriental royal ideology see Mowinckel, *He that Cometh*, E. T. Blackwell, Oxford and Abingdon, New York 1956, pp. 21–95, and Ringgren, *The Messiah in the Old Testament*, SBT 1.18, 1956, pp. 41–6.

60. Ringgren, *The Messiah*, p. 9.

61. On Ps. 2 see above, pp. 74f.

62. Quoted from II DV 6f., I D 23f.,; cf. II K VI 33f.; see G. R. Driver, *Canaanite Myths and Legends*, T. & T. Clark, Edinburgh 1956, pp. 47, 53, 59.

63. Hebrew *šālōm*, etymologically 'wholeness', is traditionally translated by 'peace'; however, it has a much broader sense connoting the happiness and harmony that obtain in a well-ordered covenant relationship. In Ps. 72 the emphasis is tilted towards the 'fertility' side of 'peace' (cf. v.3, 'The mountains bear "peace" for the people'); cf. also Ps. 147.14; Jer. 25.37; and see further Pedersen's treatment of the concept, *Israel* I–II, pp. 263–335, esp. p. 316.

64. Up to this point we have largely followed Mowinckel's understanding of the Psalms, as presented in *Psalmenstudien* II and *The Psalms*. We have now come to a point where there is considerable disagreement among members of the 'Scandinavian school'. On one side stand Engnell, 'The 'Ebed Yahweh Songs and the Suffering Messiah in "Deutero-Isaiah" ', *BJRL* 31, 1948, pp. 54–93; Widengren, 'Konungens vistelse i dödsriket', *SEA* 10, 1945, pp. 66–81; G. W. Ahlström, *Psalm 89. Eine Liturgie aus dem Ritual des leidenden Königs*, Lund 1959. The other side is represented by Mowinckel's rejection of the theory in *The Psalms* I, pp. 244ff. Our own view of the cultic suffering of the king in Jerusalem, presented in the following pages, is deeply indebted to Johnson, *Sacral Kingship*, pp. 102–28. Cf. also J. H. Grønbaek, 'Kongens Kultiske funktion i det foreksilske Israel', *DTT* 20, 1957, pp. 1–16.

65. C. J. Gadd, 'Babylonian Myth and Ritual', in Hooke (ed.), *Myth and Ritual*, pp. 53f.

66. This is the same figure we identified on p. 64 above as the *urigallu*-priest.

67. Ringgren, *Messiah*, ch. IV, offers an analysis of Pss. 18, 22, 49, 69, 86, 88, 116 and 118, and shows that they may have been employed in the drama of the New Year Festival.

68. Johnson, *Sacral Kingship*, pp. 111ff.

69. Ibid., pp. 116–23.

70. However, some OT passages do seem to refer to a blow on the cheek (with a staff!) as an important rite in the cultic suffering of the king in Jerusalem: Micah 5.1; Lam. 3.1, 30; cf. II Sam. 7.14; Ps. 89.32; Isa. 10.5.

71. See above, pp. 63ff., and Ringgren, *Faith of the Psalmists*, pp. xvi–xviii.

72. The fact that this ritual expresses the king's utter dependence on the god – he receives his entire authority from him, and only from him – reveals what is in reality a striking similarity between the Babylonian ritual and conceptions about the Israelite king which we find in the Psalms. On this theocentric motif see Ringgren, op. cit., pp. 27–36.

73. E.g. Bentzen, *King and Messiah*, ET Lutterworth and Allenson, Naperville 1955, 2nd ed., Blackwell, Oxford, 1970, pp. 29ff.; Mowinckel, *The Psalms* I, pp. 244ff.

74. Bentzen, op. cit., pp. 78f.

75. Johnson, *Sacral Kingship*, p. 106 n. 4.

76. See the suggestions in Stolz, op. cit., pp. 88f.

77. For Stolz's treatment of myth and hymn see ibid., pp. 12ff.; he understands myth as a magical understanding of reality, whereas the hymn (pp. 80f.) is held to be a thankful acknowledgment by the community that they have experienced the confirmation of the reality of the myth in external history. This is the basis for Stolz's distinction between the creation myth as myth proper and the motif of the battle with the nations as a hymnic motif (pp. 92f.). Stolz maintains that with lamentation the situation is radically different: the worshippers are seen to acknowledge the breakdown of their mythical understanding of reality under the pressure of external reality. Thus in the time of crisis they address themselves directly to the highest god in lament and prayer (pp. 122f.). In order to accommodate his generalizations to the material, Stolz is forced to introduce a razor-sharp distinction between those laments which must have figured in the cultic drama and the psalms of lamentation proper, which he interprets in terms of contemporary history (p. 122, n.14). Such a distinction can hardly be helpful in the interpretation of the OT Psalms.

78. See above, n.72.

79. Johnson, op. cit., pp. 139f.

80. Thus Mowinckel, *The Psalms* I, p. 182 n.195. Widengren advocates a more positive view of the concept of magic in *Religionsphänomenologie*, pp. 8–10.

81. K. E. Løgstrup, former Professor of Ethics and Philosophy of Religion at the University of Aarhus, writes: 'Forgiveness does not consist in our letting the other person know that we are able to forgive him. This would be the same as to make him the victim of our superiority or affection. If this is what forgiveness means, he would probably, if he is not completely depraved, much prefer to remain the object of our hate or resentment. How then do we know that we have been forgiven? This we know from

the other person's conduct toward us. How must he conduct himself in order that we may know? There is no general answer to that question, because such conduct may mean all kinds of things. It all depends upon the circumstances. For example: there may be forgiveness in a reprimand or in a condemnation of our failure, provided that in and with that reprimand or condemnation the other person is in fact re-establishing his relationship with us. But we still ask, how can we know that there is forgiveness in his reprimand and condemnation, and that it is not just a plain case of self-justification on his part?

The answer is that we simply interpret his reprimand and his condemnation of our failure in this way. It is a matter of interpretation because, strictly speaking, a verification of his sincerity is impossible. Our interpretation cannot be tested in a manner which does not involve the interpretation itself. We must interpret, there is no way to avoid it', *The Ethical Demand*, Fortress Press, Philadelphia 1971, pp.228f.

82. See II Kings 25; Jer. 52.

83. The Hebrew text is corrected in accordance with the Syriac and Aramaic translation (see H. Gottlieb, *A Study on the Text of Lamentations*, Aarhus 1978, p. 46).

4 Myth in the Prophetic Literature

1. It would however be too restrictive simply to define the prophets as spokesmen, since oral proclamation was only one of several options that were open to them in communicating their message to their contemporaries. However, this mode of communication lent itself most easily to recording and preservation for posterity, and it was through his choice of words that the prophet revealed his relationship to cult and myth.

2. Cf. Amos 3.1; Hos. 13.4; Micah 6.4, etc.

3. Hosea refers here to an act of apostasy which occurred when the desert tribes encountered the fertility religion on Moabite soil; cf. Num. 25. 'Ba'al' has here been replaced by the derogatory '*bōšet*' (Hebr. 'shame', 'shameful thing', here 'outrage'), as in Jer. 3.24; this, of course, reduces Ba'al to a caricature of a bestower of fertility (see below). Cf. the use of *Beth-'āven* for *Bethel* (p. 102).

4. The Scandinavian school (see above, p. 62) has also left its imprint on modern prophetic research. Among other things, various scholars have attempted to draw out the consequences of the relationship of OT prophecy to the rest of Near Eastern culture. See especially in this connection the chapter on 'Prophets and Prophetism' in Ivan Engnell's *Critical Essays on the Old Testament*, ET 1970, pp. 123–79.

5. Mowinckel gave *Psalmenstudien* III the subtitle *Kultprophetie und prophetische Psalmen*, thus paving the way for a new understanding of the relationship between the Psalms and the prophetic literature. See K. Jeppesen, *Profeti og protest*, Aarhus 1971.

6. The prophets felt free to protest against both the officials of the cult (e.g. Micah 3.11) and its rites (e.g. Isa. 1.10ff.); however this does not necessarily mean that they rejected the cult in principle.

7. Cf. Mowinckel's interpretation of Ps. 95 in his Norwegian translation of the OT (see p. 130 n. 12); cf. also *Psalmenstudien* II, pp. 152ff., and esp. *Psalmenstudien* III, p. 40. On the phrase 'today' see above, p. 64.

8. See above, pp. 82f. The fact that the temple may be considered the 'resting-place' is evident from Ps. 132.14; see further above pp. 83ff.

9. Aage Bentzen's rendering of Ps. 42.5, *Fortolkning til de gammeltestamentlige Salmer*, Copenhagen 1940, p. 234.

10. Cf. Ps. 95; see above, p. 96.

11. On the other hand, it is of no great importance for a work of this kind whether or not the individual oracles can be traced back to the prophet whose name the writing itself bears. There is thus no reason for us here to discuss the possibility of a Deuteronomistic background for e.g. Amos 2.9f. and parallels (see p. 94). See further below notes 17–19.

12. This is Engnell's view; see e.g. 'Profetismens ursprung och uppkomst', *RoB* 8, 1949, pp. 1–18, esp. pp. 14ff.; cf. the note in 'Prophets and Prophetism', *Critical Essays*, p. 123, and the section on Amos in 'The Figurative Language of the Old Testament', ibid., pp. 281–4.

13. E.g. H. Gottlieb, 'Amos und Jerusalem', *VT* 17, 1967, pp. 430–63, esp. p. 437.

14. See the cursing of the nations in e.g. Amos 1–2 and Isa. 13–23.

15. As expressed in Isa. 6, the theme of 'hardening' is difficult to grasp if one more or less unconsciously holds a static conception of God, i.e., a God without moods. In the book of Isaiah, however, the theme of the hardening of hearts appears right alongside the concept of righteousness (see pp. 121f. below), and a thorough-going account of Isaiah's theology accordingly demands that some sort of relationship be envisioned between these two apparently contradictory ideas.

16. There is some question as to how much strength the Hebrew verb *pittā* is to be accorded in translation. In the translation of Jer. 20.7 offered here we have attempted to play on the fact that the verb can be used of the seduction of a virgin, as in Ex. 22.15. The same *double entendre* has been attempted in our translation of Hos. 2.16f. (see above, p. 110).

17. It was a leading opinion of earlier scholars, and is still maintained by many, that the proclamation of salvation was a secondary modification of actual prophecy, whose function was seen as the announcement of judgment. Wellhausen e.g. held that the end of the book of Amos (9.11ff.) reveals 'roses and lavender instead of blood and iron', *Die Kleinen Propheten*, Berlin [4]1963, p. 96. On the end of Amos see further E. Hammershaimb, *The Book of Amos: A Commentary*, ET Blackwell, Oxford and Schocken Books, New York 1970, pp. 135ff.

18. Micah 4.1–4 (cf. Isa. 2.2–4) is so closely related to such Zion psalms as Pss. 46 and 48 (see pp. 73ff.), that the text must in any event be regarded as of pre-exilic date.

19. Isa. 4 is a text of whose originality the majority of scholars have their doubts; however, as we mentioned in n. 11 above, this is of no great importance for the purpose of our investigation. It could well be the case that the contents of this chapter are intended to represent a sort of extension of the so-called 'real' proclamation which is to be found in e.g. Isa. 28–9.

In this connection we should also like to emphasize the use made of the concept of righteousness (cf. p. 121).

20. Yet a third possibility is the conjecture that such a message may have been thought to be either offensive or meaningless at a later stage in the development of the tradition of the book of Hosea.

21. Cf. F. Hvidberg, *Weeping and Laughter in the Old Testament*, ET 1962, pp. 98–100.

22. O. Hvidberg-Hansen, 'Die Vernichtung des goldenen Kalbes und der ugaritische Ernteritus'. *AcOr* 33, 1971, pp. 5–46.

23. I AB III, 8; ET as in Hvidberg, op. cit., p. 35; cf. *NERT*, p. 219. On the problem in question see G. Widengren, *Sakrales Königtum im alten Testament und im Judentum*, Stuttgart 1955, pp. 69ff. An unclear passage in the book of Amos may possibly be read: 'As the god of Dan lives' (Amos 8.14).

24. This is exploited to ironic effect in the Elijah cycle (I Kings 18.27); note that Isa. 51 revives the use of the summons to awaken (v.17), but is directed against Jerusalem (as the collective representative of the people?); the city was previously forced to drain the 'cup of wrath' and is now to return to life. There is no doubt that a complex of mythological conceptions is operative somewhere in the background here.

25. The concept of the revival of the god is also evident in e.g. 'Inanna's Descent into the Nether World', *ANET*, pp. 52–7; some scholars hold with F. Stolz, *Strukturen und Figuren im Kult von Jerusalem*, BZAW 118, 1970, pp. 25–9, that the death rite of the goddess is described here. If in the Near Eastern fertility cult not only the fertility god but also his consort were held to have descended into the nether world, this would explain the transference of this characteristic to the people (i.e. as Yahweh's consort).

26. See above, pp. 108ff. and n. 17; we can see no reason why the existing conclusion of the book of Hosea should be regarded as inauthentic.

27. The opposite conception is maintained by Geo Widengren in 'Early Hebrew Myths and their Interpretation' in *Myth, Ritual and Kingship*, ed. S. H. Hooke, OUP 1958, pp. 149–203, esp. pp. 182f.

28. *Aramaic Papyri of the Fifth Century BC*, ed. and trans. A. Cowley, OUP 1923, reprinted Osnabrück 1967, text no. 22.1, pp. 124f.; cf. *NERT*, pp. 255f.

29. The definition of *hieros gamos* given here is an indirect quotation from the introduction to H. Ringgren's article, 'Hieros gamos i Egypten, Sumer och Israel', *RoB* 18, 1959, pp. 23–51. See also H. G. May, 'The Fertility Cult in Hosea', *AJSL* 48, 1932, pp. 73–98.

30. Our rendering of *kallōt* follows a suggestion of L. Rost, 'Erwägungen zu Hosea 4, 13f.', *Das kleine Credo und andere Studien zum Alten Testament*, Heidelberg 1965, pp. 53ff., esp. pp. 54–6. It is possible that the maidens here referred to are participants in the variety of rite that Herodotus (I, 199) termed 'the most outrageous of all the laws of the Babylonians'.

31. The text of Hos. 9.2 presents some translation difficulties. *yir'e* is taken, following a suggestion of H. S. Nyberg (*Studien zum Hoseabuche*, Uppsala 1935, p. 68) to signify 'to be everyone's friend and comrade, to be friends with everyone'.

32. Since the institution of marriage in the West is remote both in theory

and practice from the customs of ancient Israel, it is difficult to capture in a translation all the nuances of those texts which depict the relation of Yahweh to Israel as a form of marraige. In the translation here attempted we have chosen to imply that the divine virtues of *ṣedeq*, *mišpaṭ* and so forth constitute the bride-price.

33. Hos. 1–3. To attempt to discuss the relationship between the two accounts of marriage present in chs. 1 and 3 would be beyond the purposes of this work. When in 1.2 the woman is called *'ešet zᵉnūnīm*, the implication is probably that she has at one time had a professional part in the rites of the *hieros gamos* which Hosea opposes.

34. On the rendering of *mᵉpattē* (2.14, Hebrew 2.16) see above, n. 16. The expression *wᵉ dibbartī al-libbāh*, literally 'and he will speak to her heart', is decisive for the tone of the verse. The question is whether Yahweh will speak lovingly or chastisingly to the people; we have here opted for the latter, since the heart was then regarded as the seat of the rational faculty.

35. Pedersén, *Israel* I–II, p. 463.

36. *'ānā* (2.15, Hebrew 2.17) could conceivably mean 'sing' (RSV) in this context, and its usual meaning, 'answer', is also a possibility; cf. in our translation 'answer', with an undertone of advocacy (vv. 21f., Heb. 23f.). Here in continuation of the sense of v. 14 we have chosen the meaning 'to be bent down, over', which literally means 'to take a lower position'.

37. With these words Jeremiah reveals his ignorance of Canaanite religion, since the stone was the male and the tree the female symbol, whereas in Hebrew these words have the opposite gender. See e.g. E. Nielsen, 'The Righteous and the Wicked in Habbaqquq', *StTh* 6, 1952, pp. 54–78, esp. p. 63. Incidentally, Ba'al also becomes feminine when he is referred to as *bōšet* (cf. p. 95 and n. 3).

38. The two riddling names here are difficult; there is perhaps a play on the word *'ōhel*, 'tent', which is occasionally used as a synonym for 'temple'. Thus the passage may conceivably be taken to suggest that the true temple lies in Jerusalem.

39. The single Hebrew verb *zākar* is taken to mean 'to recall' in v. 60, (cf. Jer. 2.2, p. 111 above), and 'acknowledge' in v. 61. 'Memory' does not consist merely of mental activity, but also of the consequences to which such activity leads.

40. We ought perhaps to mention that some of the elements of the old fertility religion are preserved in poetic form in the literature of the OT, specifically in the Song of Solomon. This collection contains some survivals of a cultic lyric belonging to the rites of the *hieros gamos*; they were most probably included in the canon because they still retained an aura of sanctity, and because, like the prophetic texts with which we have been concerned here, it was possible to interpret them as if they described the relationship of Yahweh to Israel. Here we should merely like to stress only a few characteristics which point to the original milieu of these texts: the woman *seeks* her beloved bridegroom, and is prevented by night-watchmen (e.g. 3.2ff.); she is depicted as beautiful and alluring, with the emphasis on her erotic attributes (4.1ff., 6.4ff., 7.1ff.); and finally, the woman's paramour

also possesses divine beauty (5.10ff.). Cf. H. Ringgren, *Das hohe Lied*, ATD 16, 1962.

41. Cf. Joel 3.16 (pp. 118f.).

42. It is possible that Hosea regarded the kings of the Northern Kingdom as a punishment from Yahweh (cf. 13.11). The conclusion of the book of Amos also points to a future where the Davidic royal house is reinstated, but both this text (Amos 9.11ff.) and Hos. 3.5 are often held to be late additions. This is a tenable point of view, even if one does not share Wellhausen's opinion on the matter (see n. 17). See for example, A. S. Kapelrud, *Central Ideas in Amos*, Oslo 1956, pp. 56ff.

43. I. Engnell, 'The 'Ebed Yahweh Songs and the Suffering Messiah in Deutero-Isaiah', *BJRL* 31, 1948, pp. 54ff.

44. Nikkal and the Kathirat, 7.1.7; see G. R. Driver, *Canaanite Myths and Legends*, 1956, pp. 124f. The Ugaritic word *ǧlmt*, which corresponds to *'almā*, is used here; we should note that it can also be used to designate a female divinity; E. Hammershaimb, 'The Immanuel Sign', *Some Aspects of Old Testament Prophecy*, Copenhagen 1966, pp. 7–28; H. Gottlieb, *VT* 17, 1967, pp. 54ff.

45. There is an obvious connection here between the Hebrew *yōlēdā* and the Ishtar designation *muallidatu*; the latter is presumably the name Herodotus (I, 199) records as Mylitta.

46. It is obvious that the temple of Shiloh was a well-known ruin in Jeremiah's day.

47. 'North' bears connotations of both divine salvation and destruction (see pp. 118f.). The fact that the temple was regarded as the centre of both the world and the country was suggested above, p. 68; see Mircea Eliade, *The Sacred and the Profane*, ET 1959, ch. 2. See also p. 130 n. 24 above.

48. Zech. 14 is a relatively late text with a clearly apocalyptic character; cf. B. Otzen, *Studien über Deuterosacharja*, Copenhagen 1964, pp. 199ff.

49. In Joel 3.10 (Hebrew 4.10) formulaic language is obviously being used. The words that describe the start of the war are the same as those used in Micah 4.3 and Isa. 2.4 to describe the end of a war, only in reverse.

50. See above, p. 114; it is only possible to treat it as a name in Isa. 8.8.

51. Cf. Joel 2.1f., 11. It is essential to realize that precisely the same expression is used in a description of the day of Yahweh, directed against strangers, in Isa. 13.6; cf. above p. 97, and esp. Amos 5.18.

52. See e.g. Zech 14.; cf. also p. 118 above and n. 48.

53. These words form a link with another type of formulaic language, that which was employed during a sacred procession up to Zion (see pp. 82ff.). This language is frequently employed by Deutero-Isaiah (e.g. at 41.3ff.). It is clear that Isa. 51.11 is formulaic language; since the same words are used in a different context in Isa. 35.10.

INDEX OF BIBLICAL REFERENCES